Jew and Improved

Jew and Improved

HOW CHOOSING TO BE CHOSEN
MADE ME A BETTER MAN

Benjamin Errett
Illustrations by Sarah Lazarovic

HarperCollins*PublishersLtd*

Published by HarperCollins Publishers Ltd

First Edition

Licensee gratefully acknowledges USC Shoah Foundation Institute for Visual
History and Education, University of Southern California, for allowing us to
use the testimony of Helena Lazarovic.

HarperCollins books may be purchased for educational, business,
or sales promotional use through our Special Markets Department.

HarperCollins Publishers Ltd
2 Bloor Street East, 20th Floor
Toronto, Ontario, Canada
M4W 1A8

www.harpercollins.ca

Library and Archives Canada Cataloguing in Publication
Errett, Benjamin, 1978–
Jew and improved : how choosing to be chosen made
me a better man / Benjamin Errett.

ISBN 978-1-55468-427-4

1. Errett, Benjamin, 1978—Humor. 2. Jewish way of life—Humor.
3. Spiritual life—Judaism–Humor. 4. Jewish converts from Christianity—
Canada—Biography. 5. Canadian wit and humor (English). I. Title.

BM755.E77 2010   296.7'14092   C2009-905716-6

Mixed Sources
Cert no. SW-COC-001271
© 1996 FSC
FSC

Printed and bound in Canada
DWF 9 8 7 6 5 4 3 2 1

For Sarah, obviously

Contents

SARAH'S CLASS SKETCHBOOK

Rush to Judgment

Preparing for formal acceptance into the covenant of Judaism is like preparing for a job interview. You need to be confident, articulate and well versed in the history of the organization you hope to join. You also need to wear the appropriate necktie.

"What do you think?" I asked Sarah, performing an unnecessary pirouette in my navy blue suit.

"The suit's good, but I'm not sure about the tie."

I knew the orange paisley wouldn't pass muster, as we'd had the conversation before. Orange and blue are opposite each other on the colour wheel, I'd argued in an appeal to my fiancée's formal training in the arts. Her rebuttal, as unnuanced as it was irrefutable, was that it looked cheesy. As I returned to my closet, I took solace in the fact that she approved of the majority of my neckwear. Our aesthetics were nearly identical, and after today, God willing, our religions would be as well. I selected a light blue tie with pinpoint white polka dots and returned to Sarah's office on the second floor of our house.

"Sharpie doo!" she exclaimed, an expression she'd picked up from her Bronx-born grandmother.

"And you'll notice they're the colours of Israel," I said. "Dress for the job you want, right?"

I hadn't always wanted this job; for most of my life, I was quite happy to be unemployed, spiritually speaking. But when Sarah and I got engaged, I decided joining her tribe was the right thing to do. Beyond that slogan for Quaker Oats, I couldn't quite articulate why I wanted to do this. Sure, it made her parents happy, but I'd like to think I had them on side from the beginning. I knew I was searching for something, though I had no clear idea what that something was. At that early stage, I didn't even consider that I'd be dragging Sarah along on this quest for meaning, whether she wanted to go or not. While I realized I'd eventually have to explain myself to my family, our friends and my new religious leaders, I didn't consider that my wife-to-be would have to do the same. More fundamentally, I didn't even have the right route for the journey: I thought I was going from Christianity to Judaism, where I'd arrive to find Sarah. In fact, we were both starting at the same religion-free place, and we had no way of knowing where we'd end up.

But I went ahead and got both of us into this—this year of synagogue attendance, weekly classes, intensive Hebrew, immersion in the contradictions of a major world religion, and now this morning's appointment—and at that moment, Sarah was getting the both of us into a borrowed Honda Civic.

I was, as usual, running late, and she wasn't about to miss our appointment with the panel of rabbis who would be considering my application. Formally known as a *beit din,* or house of judgment, the elders who interviewed converts also comprised the religious court that arbitrated disputes, handed out kosher designations and granted divorces.

When we first learned about the *beit din* in our Jewish education classes, I pictured the venue as Superman's Fortress of Solitude, the ice palace where Kryptonian sages advised Christopher Reeve. Over time, my mental image had evolved to the setting of the Albert Brooks movie *Defending Your Life*—which, if not more accurate, was at least more Jewish than Marlon Brando in a silver jumpsuit. In actuality, the adjudication took place in a squat, suburban office building, around a boardroom table.

We parked the car and made our way into the building. It was a sunny January day, the sort on which the dirty snowbanks make the sky look that much bluer.

"Again, it's the colours of Israel," I said to Sarah. "Must be a good omen."

Her teeth chattered in reply. She was too bundled up to hear me, something I should have expected. The Lazarovics and cold weather have never gotten along. Her family fled Montreal in the early 1980s in part because, after years of freezing, Sarah's mother, Debbie, had cracked. As a result, Sarah and her two younger sisters were raised in sunny Boca Raton, Florida, where cardigan weather is enough to warrant complaints. As a result, her move back to Canada as a university student was a reintroduction to—and re-education in—the realities of climate.

By now she understood the weather, but that didn't mean she liked it. We made it inside before she could make this point once again.

The office resembled a daycare. We soon learned that another function of the *beit din* is to answer thorny questions raised about faith and adoption by Jewish parents, which may necessitate examining the children in question. The parents were subtly showing off their new acquisitions by loudly praising them and explaining their plight to half-listening seatmates. I made a point of tuning them out.

We didn't want kids, at least not yet, though we had often mentioned them when fielding queries about conversion. In our families there were devoted Catholics, occasional synagogue-goers, dabbling Buddhists and committed agnostics, but all were united in their desire to see another bundle of joy brought into this world. If my conversion to Judaism was presented as a way to make that happen, then it made sense to my grandmothers. We'd want to raise our children in one faith, I'd say, and the unprompted discussion of children worked wonders. This strategy would only be of use with our elders, we soon realized. Among our peer group of delayed adolescents, it was slightly unsettling. Better to tell friends I was doing it—*we* were doing it—for ourselves, even if we didn't really know why.

Now, sitting in the waiting room, I realized that I did need to know. This was the point at which I'd be asked for the final time. That was an anxiety-inducing thought, and I instinctively looked to Sarah. She too looked worried as she scanned an article about the Jewish contribution to pickled foods in America. After seven years together, I knew she wasn't actually fretting about my interview, or about pickles. Rather, her default facial expression was a worried frown, a tic that was first publicly acknowledged when she was eight.

"Sarah seems so sad all the time. Is anything wrong?" a concerned neighbour asked Debbie.

"What do you mean?"

"We see her walking home from school and she looks like she's about to cry."

"Who smiles when they're walking home from school by themselves?" Sarah asked when her mother told me that story. "Only a crazy person."

"She's just like her father," Debbie said. "That's just her demeanour. It's hard to get them to crack a smile."

Some consternation before my judgment would have been understandable, though we had heard from family, friends and fellow classmates that once your rabbi makes an appointment with the *beit din,* you're pretty much guaranteed a pass. Any flaws in your conversion would have long since been spotted, and though there was a time when the failure rate was higher, all parties realized it was a better use of everyone's time to fully screen all the applicants. That said, we'd also heard horror stories. We had travelled to Israel the year before, and there our highly irritating guide told us that a friend had flunked out on the first question.

"Where is God?" the rabbis had asked, and she instinctively pointed upward. Cue the trapdoor: in Judaism, God is everywhere—or possibly nowhere, as our books and teachers suggested without too much elaboration. What matters is actions, not beliefs, says one Jewish axiom. As well, Reform

Jews can see the events of the Bible as elaborate metaphor: there weren't really a burning bush and stone tablets and a pillar of salt and all that.

I was never sure enough to be an atheist, but I certainly qualified as an agnostic. This, I was relieved to learn, was more or less permitted. One of the Jewish names for God is Hidden of Hiddens, so it only makes sense that He would be mysterious. That said, I wasn't about to bring that up today. Though I'd rather make three right turns than a left, I wouldn't mention that to my driving instructor. But what if I were asked?

"Benjamin?" the rabbi asked. "We're ready for you."

In Our Beginning

The first time I met Sarah, I thought she was crazy. She had come into the offices of *The McGill Daily* with a story we just *had* to cover. As the student paper's editor-in-chief—technically, I was the "coordinating editor," as we were a non-hierarchical organization, which was an oxymoron, but I digress—I listened to her tale of an abusive landlord with a history of defrauding Montreal students, focusing more on the incredible speed at which she spoke and her frantic hand gestures than on the actual story. We never followed it up.

Despite that snub, she joined the paper as culture editor later that semester. As such, Sarah was party to my all-staff invitation to partake in the game of squash. At the time, I was a biology major in the midst of applying to medical school. I'd decided that if I were to spend the next four to eight years of my life in academia, I should take up the sport of brainiacs. I had many takers, Sarah among them. I later learned that she considered that our first date.

"I don't know about this guy. He wore shorts and had pasty white legs!" she told her roommates after the game, which I won.

"Eww!" they exclaimed—unfairly, as it was an athletic activity played in the dead of winter. Obviously, tanned legs would have been much creepier.

We went on a series of kinda-sorta dates after that—walks on Mount Royal, participation in a Comics Jam, a bike ride to the Biodome. I wasn't quite sure at first if this was a friendship or a romance—in retrospect, I was oblivious—but by the time of our eighth date, when Sarah wore a T-shirt that read "*Besame Mucho*," I'd figured it out.

That was in May of 2001, when I was earning the final credits of my academic career in a summer course called Existentialism and Buddhism. It was taught by a graduate student who wore board shorts, and it represented the liberal arts education I'd dreamed of while pipetting mitochondria in the concrete bunker that was the biology building. My roommate, Ryan, and I sat at the back of the 1920s-era classroom, snickering at the teacher. We'd mark the end of each class with an ice cream cone at the nearby engineering building. In retrospect, it seems so idyllic because I was in love. Sarah would occasionally meet me after class, and we'd bike around town, visiting friends, sitting in cafés and avoiding the squash courts.

At the time, Sarah worked at Global Action Network, where she was the communications coordinator. The animal rights organization's tenets had very little in common with those of my future wife, but she dutifully argued against the proposed dolphinarium at the Granby Zoo on local call-in shows. I was accepted to McGill's medical school, and while this news was welcome, it also filled me with dread, especially when I looked at the course syllabus. Four months of vacation the first year, followed by three, followed by . . . none? I began to realize that a doctor who was put off by the lack of summer vacation in medical school was hardly the person you wanted hovering over you with a scalpel. All this was quite agonizing to contemplate—if I didn't go to medical school, what would I do?—but the aforementioned love in my life was a perfect distraction.

May lazed into June and the final course of my undergraduate career came to an end. As a graduation gift, my father had generously offered to bankroll a summer's travels, though the combination of Sarah's presence in my life and the city in full bloom made me reluctant to go anywhere. For the first time in memory I had no real commitments, a condition that led me to create a series of increasingly surreal websites, including Existential Pud, which applied my superficial knowledge of Sartre et al. to the inane wax-paper comics that accompanied Dubble Bubble bubble gum. I had just purchased the domain name for Marshall, Marshall, Marshall, a site that was to examine the confluences between Marshall McLuhan's media theories and *The Brady Bunch*—and perhaps cement my slide into digital dadaism—when I received a job offer at a Toronto-based national newspaper.

Up until that time, I had successfully split my attention between science—a subject I mastered without much joy—and journalism, something I lived and breathed but decided wasn't serious enough for a career. In my first summers home from university, I'd worked in a lab, killing rodents in the name of medical research. (When Sarah learned this, her lack of compassion for the poor Norway rats made clear that she didn't belong at Global Action Network.) By my third year of university I had realized that my lunchtime visits to the international newsstand were the highlights of my lab jobs, so I applied for an internship at the country's oldest magazine. When I started there, it had just become an insert in a national newspaper. My duties included fact-checking the crossword puzzle, which wasn't nearly as bloody as my laboratory job. Things came to a head when we received an angry letter asking how, exactly, the letters "GST" answered a clue about a measure of time; didn't we mean to abbreviate Greenwich Mean Time? In truth, we probably did, but the largest dictionary I could find saved my reputation by including an entry for Greenwich Sidereal Time, a complex phenomenon I pretended to understand.

That retroactive attention to detail led to a cryptic invitation from the paper's editor the following June—something about "some work for you," an offer that might very well consist of some boxes that needed lifting, I'd told Sarah. In fact, I was asked to fill in for a junior editor during the month of July. I would be responsible for Avenue, an award-winning daily visual page that I was supremely underqualified to oversee. I had never been published in a national paper, let alone edited at one.

Sarah agreed I'd be foolish not to give it a try, especially given the ridiculous work keeping me in Montreal. Less than three months into our life together, we decided to live apart. The specifics of the discussion are hazy, perhaps because there wasn't one. Obviously, I'd do this, and she'd visit, and we'd take it as it came. Sarah was in the midst of a complicated academic arrangement—she was a special student at McGill (the most special student of all, I told her) and was working toward a studio arts degree at Concordia—and would be in Montreal for at least another year. As I was due to begin medical school at McGill in late August, we would be back together in about a month. If she came to visit and I returned the favour, we wouldn't have to spend more than two weeks apart at a stretch. I packed up my stuff, returned to my father's house in Toronto and joined the world of the employed.

A month came and went. I quickly learned that my superiors were quite impressed by a little bit of advance planning. I had to attend a highly intimidating 11 a.m. news meeting and send my page by 4—hours that any college student could manage, especially one who could draw up an editorial calendar. For this I was paid an intern's salary, but the novelty was payment enough. Just seeing headlines being written as I passed by newsroom computers was exciting—tomorrow's news today!—and made the whole thing feel like a journalism fantasy camp. As August arrived, I guessed that the previous occupant of my cubicle had no intention of returning. (When she published a tell-all magazine feature a month later rating the sex appeal of the paper's senior editors, my hunch was confirmed.) I also realized that my contract was about to expire, setting the stage for my first-ever business negotiation. I asked to meet the editor-in-chief.

"So, as you know, this is my last week here," I said.

"It is?" He was distracted, though to be fair, I was probably in the bottom percentile of his concerns.

11

"Yes. I don't know if you have anyone else ready to take over Avenue"—this was my attempt at both flattery and a bluff—"but I'd be willing to extend my contract."

"Aren't you off to medical school in the fall?" the editor asked.

"I have been accepted, but I like this work and would be willing to defer for a year," I said, immediately realizing that I didn't know *if* I could defer, and more to the point, I didn't know I officially wanted to defer until I heard myself saying it. I also realized that it would have been smarter to be offered the job than to volunteer for it. And if he said yes, then Sarah and I couldn't pretend we weren't in a long-distance relationship. While my mind was fumbling through this series of conclusions, the editor looked mildly amused at the kid who'd been here for four weeks and was trying to make him an offer he couldn't refuse.

"How about a one-year contract?" he said, smiling.

"All right," I replied quickly, trying to strengthen my bargaining position, "but I'd like to be paid what the previous occupant of the job was getting, not an intern's salary." He found this last-minute bravado even more entertaining.

"Our interns make very good money!" he said. I smiled back, trying to appear to be in on the joke.

"Do you know how expensive it is to live in downtown Toronto?" I said. "Especially with the high taxes we're always writing about."

A week later I was handed a contract at a considerably higher pay rate. This real-world stuff wasn't so hard, I thought, at least until I called McGill's medical school and asked about the deferral policy. "There isn't one, except in extreme circumstances," the receptionist told me.

"What if I were taking French lessons?" I asked. I'd tried and failed to master Quebec's official language while attending school there. It wasn't mandatory for medical students to be bilingual, but perhaps the lessons I had yet to enrol in could be deemed extreme. "Would that be sufficient?"

"No."

Soon afterward, I was summoned to meet with the board of admissions, ostensibly regarding some confusion over late submission of my previous term's marks. I took a Friday off work, rented a car and headed down the 401, eager to see Sarah and expecting to have to explain the whereabouts of my grade in Buddhism. When I arrived at the meeting, I found that that was only one of their concerns. Did I call to ask about deferrals, an admissions officer demanded.

Suddenly, I realized that the relatively small freshman class meant there was no anonymity. I did, I said.

Was I serious about French lessons?

I was.

Was I completely committed to attending classes that fall?

As I had just signed a year-long contract, I said no.

Then my interrogators switched to good-cop mode, graciously inviting me to reapply in the future in exchange for a withdrawal of my present enrolment. I didn't want to give up the option, but it was quite clear I had no choice. I realized this must be how criminals feel when the option of a plea bargain is raised—not the most desirable result, but better than spending another moment in that room. As I walked numbly out of the building for what I imagined would be the last time, I realized that I wasn't in limbo anymore. It felt good to have made a decision, even if I wasn't really the one who had made it and I wasn't entirely sure it was the right one.

That spirit of momentousness permeated the weekend. Sarah wanted to talk about my telephone demeanour, or lack thereof. I didn't like talking on the phone with her, a proclivity I assured her was based entirely on my hatred of the technology—the crick in your neck, the stilted recounting of the day's happenings, the charade that you're able to live and love in two places at once.

"Does that mean you want to break up?" Sarah asked.

"Well, maybe it would be the right thing to do," I replied. I thought I was being logical. Sarah insisted I was being childish.

We were both right, of course: a long-distance love affair is completely illogical, which is why only grown-ups can pull it off. To chalk up our time together as a summer fling seemed the grown-up thing to do, I maintained. Painful, but necessary. I was perhaps still numb from the interrogation. I had no idea what I was talking about.

Did I love her? Sarah asked.

I did.

Did I see a future for us if we stayed in the same city?

I did.

Then why would I let geography and a hatred of phones ruin that?

She was right.

I returned to Toronto feeling much smarter than when I'd left. Now, everything about my life in limbo had been dealt with: I was starting a new chapter on firm ground, knowing exactly what was what. I moved into an apartment with Jason, a fellow *Daily*ite who'd become a business reporter at the paper, and began treating my job like the beginning of a career.

September 11 happened shortly thereafter, a day that seemed to change things much more profoundly at the time than it has in retrospect. A week later, the paper was gutted by layoffs. Jason and I sat in our cubicles, exchanging emails about the carnage around us. I'd figured we were toast and had begun preparing a travel itinerary for a trip through Eastern Europe. I'd visit Sarah for a few weeks and take off from Montreal, touring the continent and figuring out what to do next. Perhaps I'd call that admissions officer's bluff and reapply to med school. Or maybe it was time to take Existential Pud down to Silicon Valley. The future was full of possibility, and it would officially start just as soon as they handed me that pink slip. But they didn't, though I was reassigned. By early afternoon, I had become one of three arts reporters left in the building.

I was immediately assigned to prepare an obituary for Mr. Dressup, a beloved children's entertainer who was about to expire. Senior editors with kids and mortgages were let go while I kept my head down in my cubicle, trying to track down the puppeteer who had created the characters of Casey and Finnegan. Why was I still there? The lack of pricey dental benefits on my contract was my naive first guess, but I later determined that the circumstances of my entry—he turned down medical school! For *this!*—played a part in my continued employment. I got in touch with Mr. Rogers's office, secured interviews with Fred Penner and Raffi, learned that Mr. Dressup's Tickle Trunk would be displayed at the Canadian Museum of Civilization and wrote the first story of my professional reporting career.

Those were the first six months of my life with Sarah. Aside from my bird course in Buddhism, we never discussed religion.

Religion, Shmeligion

When you're certain there's no God, you're an atheist. When you're not sure, you're an agnostic. When you stop considering the question altogether because it's completely irrelevant to your life, you're just like Sarah and me.

If either of us had an opinion on religion—for, against or even strenuous indifference—we would have mentioned it at some point in our first six months together. We didn't.

We arrived at this state from different backgrounds. I was baptized as a Catholic in Kingston, Ontario, and attended catechism classes in first, second and third grades at École Saint-Léon-de-Westmount in Montreal. They would separate us from our classmates of other faiths for these classes, and I remember suspecting that the Protestants among us did something much more fun than Bible study. This was never confirmed (and neither were they). I received my First Communion.

Sarah was born into the covenant of Judaism and sent to South County Jewish Community Day School in sunny Boca Raton, Florida, until the third grade. Her only distinct memories of that education involve not doubt but forgetfulness: she frequently misplaced her oversized blue glasses; she forgot her lunch on purpose to get the challah bread with cream cheese and jelly given to those without; and she wore a big tinfoil crown when she dressed up as Queen Esther during the holiday of Purim.

My family moved from Montreal to Connecticut when I was in the fourth grade, and that was effectively the end of religion in our lives. We occasionally attended services at Holy Infant Church in the town of Orange, but compared to the hundred-year-old cathedral in Montreal, the ranch-style house of worship didn't inspire the necessary awe to keep us coming back. Though my father had ostensibly converted from Protestantism to marry, he had little interest in attending Mass, and when he did, he'd always make a point of saying "Let's go get a bite to eat" before the body of Christ was offered. At the time, my mother was in the final stages of perfecting her parenting credo, which was "Do what you want; you will anyway." That was a licence to quit piano lessons, skip out of camp and stay far away from church. We became Christmas-and-Easter Catholics.

Sarah's parents were not so lax: she continued in Sunday school till the age of thirteen, when she had her *b'not mitzvah*. (I knew a bar mitzvah was the occasion on which Jewish kids received terrific presents, but I needed Sarah to explain that the girls' ceremony was a bat mitzvah and that when two girls—Sarah and Becky, her younger sister by one year—went through the rite together, it was a *b'not mitzvah*.) Videotape of this occasion survives and has been helpfully transferred to DVD, so I've been able to watch Sarah in all her awkward, pubescent glory. The after-party included a professional breakdancer, a limbo bar, a group singalong to Hammer's "2 Legit 2 Quit" and some prime examples of early-'90s hair. Battle hardened, Sarah went on to become president of the Boca Federation of Temple Youth at age sixteen.

Outside of Jesus's birthday and rebirthday, the only occasions when my family would attend church were our summer visits to our maternal grandmother in Smiths Falls, Ontario. When our parents were in the midst of a messy divorce, these visits became more frequent. There, my brother, sister and I would be dragged to the church in which our parents had been married. By mid-morning on an August Sunday, it became stifling, and I remember looking up toward the ceiling fans during silent prayer and asking that they spin just a bit faster. Desperate to pass the time, I studied the bulletin and found myself wondering why our collection plate coins went to anti-abortion groups. Did we believe in that? I asked my mother on the drive back to my grandmother's. We didn't. So why did we give money? She didn't have an answer.

Sarah's questions must have all had answers, because she doesn't remember them and they didn't stop her rapid rise through the world of adolescent Judaism. She was a youth delegate to the Union of American Hebrew Congregations' biennial convention in Washington, D.C., where Vice-President Al Gore addressed the convention. She remembers him joking that because Bill Clinton was out of the country he was effectively president. In Sunday school—a Jewish thing too, I learned—she became one of the teachers, imparting Jewish folk songs to the little ones. She briefly decided she wanted to become a cantor, the person who leads the singing at temple services. To that end, she took song-leading classes at a Jewish leadership camp in upstate New York and composed a musical about the holidays of Hanukkah and Purim. Eventually, she abandoned this dream, not because of serious philosophical differences but simply because she didn't like singing enough to make a career of it.

For my final years of high school, I moved with my father and brother to Toronto. My mother and sister moved to Vermont. None of this made much sense at the time—though I was glad the fighting was finally over—and as a result I immersed myself in schoolwork, something that I could eventually comprehend. As I was planning to major in biology at university, I took all the requisite science courses and became particularly amused by our lessons on the debates over evolution. Who were these religious cranks who argued with straight faces that God had sent angels down to hide fossils as a way of fooling scientists? There is a brief portion of adolescence when you feel like you've got the world pretty much figured out. At that point, I realized the binary choice between religion and science was a remarkably easy one.

When you learn about the Holocaust early and in extensive detail, I'm not sure that that temporary adolescent understanding of the universe ever happens. Sarah went on the March of the Living in her senior year at Atlantic High School, a grim, week-long expedition to former concentration camps across Poland followed by what is intended to be a spirit-raising week in Israel. She remembers the trip being almost entirely self-contained—staying on the bus most of the time, eating only special kosher food they brought along and hearing one of her fellow Marchers urinate into a bottle when the bus driver was unable to pull over on a remote patch of Polish highway.

I graduated from high school and entered McGill. My then-girlfriend Jennifer and I attended Easter brunch with my mother at the Queen Elizabeth Hotel. Christmas was celebrated in the most nondenominational way possible, and one year I tried to renounce the idea of gift-giving altogether. That back-fired when no one reciprocated.

Despite her father's urging that she attend his alma mater, Sarah spurned McGill in favour of Florida State University in Tallahassee. The difference between Florida's panhandle and the southeast is the difference between the Deep South and a geriatric suburb of New York City, at least in terms of Jewish population. Sarah gave up all hope of meeting a nice Jewish boy once she'd seen the two representatives of that demographic on campus. She tells a story of dating a well-meaning if ignorant stoner from Dunedin. "I just think it's cool that you're Jewish," he'd said to her after his fifth joint.

I remember asking my new roommate, Ryan, why he had a cross with footrests over his door. It was, he explained, the shape of the Orthodox cross. He was baptized in the Ukrainian church, and while he didn't believe any of it, he professed to like the ceremony of it all, not that he ever attended Mass. During our late-night contemplations of the meaninglessness of life—

he was a philosophy major, so this was practically coursework—
he would frequently cite his priest's answers to all unanswerable
questions: "Ees mystery!" he would say with an Eastern European accent and a shrug. This still seems theologically sound.

Perhaps to make up for the paucity of Judaism in Tallahassee, Sarah spent her summers in Israel. In her first year of
university, she earned money for the trip by cataloguing Jewish
films at the Adolph & Rose Levis Jewish Community Center.
She took a Hebrew course at Tel Aviv University and made vita-
min-enriched gummi bears on a kibbutz in her second summer.
She graduated in a hurry and moved to Montreal, where, to the
delight of her parents, her sister Becky had enrolled at McGill.

Becky recalls my making an erudite point about Catherine
Tekakwitha, the seventeenth-century Mohawk saint at the centre
of Leonard Cohen's *Beautiful Losers,* in a Canadian literature
tutorial we both took. I dispute this memory, as I'm pretty sure I
couldn't get more than twenty pages into that book.

Sarah took Hebrew and Middle Eastern history classes at
McGill. She also met with the chair of the Jewish Studies program to discuss a master's in Jewish-American literature. Then,
for reasons she is unable to describe, she realized she had no interest in doing a master's degree in Jewish-American literature. She
jokes that there was only so much Philip Roth a girl could take.
She applied to do a studio art degree at Concordia University.

And that's when we met. I was almost a decade removed
from religion, while her gradual withdrawal left her with little
more than a *Big Lebowski* postcard (in Hebrew) on her bedroom
wall and an obligation to attend Passover at her aunt Sandy's
house in Ottawa.

There were other remnants of faith, including one I had never even considered. Sarah was a vegetarian at university, a dietary choice that put her in a sizable minority within my university circle. I directed most of my scorn toward vegans, arguing that taking honey from bees was a perfectly proportionate response to their love of stinging us. Vegetarianism, while not fun, was much more tolerable. By the end of my university years, I had even developed a fondness for a popular brand of vegetable-based pâté. But once I left campus life and joined the working world, I began to forget about life without meat and was thus unprepared for one of Sarah's visits from Montreal.

"Upon your arrival tonight, the following menu will be served on our expansive terrace," I wrote in a mock formal email.

Savories
✡ Various cheeses and veggie pâté
✡ Grilled rainbow trout
✡ Some sort of salad
✡ Some sort of starch

Sweets
✡ Apple pie
✡ Vanilla ice cream

That was written early in the day. By the time I'd left work, got to the grocery store and surveyed the anemic, shrink-wrapped seafood offerings, I realized I had to change courses. Sarah wouldn't eat the pork skewers I had procured, but we had some frostbitten veggie burgers at home, and I figured we'd make do. When she finally arrived, numb and hungry from six hours on the dullest stretch of highway in North America, there was no time to stop her from taking a bite of what I must admit was expertly grilled pork.

"I haven't eaten anything since lunch, and all the sandwiches at Tim Hortons looked disgusting," she said, speaking at the speed that typically befuddled the elderly. "I'm so glad I waited! This fish is amazing!" She pronounced it *a-may-zing*.

"Thank you. The reason it tastes so good is that it's not fish."

"What?" she exclaimed. A half-skewer was already on the way down, so a spit-take was not an option. She ran into the apartment. I admit to finding it comical at the time; four years at a liberal university followed by immediate immersion into suburban office culture had whittled away my tolerance of self-righteous vegetarians. Sarah wasn't one of those, of course, and she ridiculed those who claimed to have become violently ill after accidentally allowing meat to cross their lips. The problems, she later told me, were that I laughed and that it was pork.

"You said it was fish!"

"That was eight hours ago! They didn't have fish at the crappy supermarket! And whoever heard of fish souvlaki anyway?"

"I don't know, but it's not funny!"

"Well, it's sort of funny."

"Dude, I've been a vegetarian for twelve years. Fish was a big step for me."

"I'm sorry," I said, not really feeling sorry, not sounding it either, and not understanding how a morsel of delectable meat could offend so deeply.

"And it was pork, too!"

"Yes . . . and?"

"Jews don't eat pork! Kosher ones, anyway!"

"But . . . you're not kosher, are you?"

"No, but that's not the point! I can't believe I just ate pork," she said, half laughing, half crying, half hitting me, half secretly wanting the rest of the skewer. That adds up to four halves, but she's a complicated lady.

Sarah rebounded with a veggie burger. Her face-first slide down the slippery slope of carnivorousness—a delicious image, I know—soon followed. As any lapsed vegetarian or kosher keeper will gladly admit, bacon is the deal-breaker. I'd call it a gateway meat, but the comparison to marijuana is unfair: people who smoke up might go on to drugs with bigger, longer-lasting highs, but there's nothing better than bacon. Before long, Sarah was ordering BLTs without hesitation.

When her school year came to an end, Sarah came to Toronto for the summer. On a friend's recommendation, she decided we should go on a Sunday morning walking tour of the formerly Jewish parts of Toronto. These had long ago given way to the Chinese parts of Toronto, and even those were in flux. Both immigrant groups had settled downtown only until they found their bearings and made some money. At that point, they'd headed north to suburbia, taking with them the best food but leaving behind the best architecture.

If it had any religious function at all, the tour served to remind us that religion was something that urbanites once observed on weekend mornings in the distant past but had now given up in favour of dim sum. See that Chinese buffet?

It used to be the Labour Lyceum, and Jewish anarchist Emma Goldman's body lay there. This community centre? Used to be a thriving synagogue. And that run-down synagogue? Well, it's still a synagogue frequented by the elderly orthodox, but who knows for how much longer. If you wanted to be devout, you should have moved to the suburbs in the early 1970s.

Sarah did manage to use her years of Hebrew training that morning, a skill I was only vaguely aware she had. It was a little bit like those movies where a family man reveals himself to have been a martial-arts expert in a past life, only Sarah was more familiar with guttural sounds than dropkicks. It seemed like an interesting skill learned for a since-abandoned career, like my ability to build models in organic chemistry. Had I given it any thought at the time, my science background might have led me to call it a vestigial structure, like the human appendix—something we carry around with us long after it has outlived its original use.

Five years later, we'd find it was actually quite handy.

The Propositions

When I asked Sarah to marry me, it wasn't a fair question. I knew her answer in advance because we'd arrived at it together three days before. Our marriage, we decided, would begin the way we wanted it to continue: with plenty of communication, on equal footing and without such silly formalities as two months' salary spent on a shard of compressed carbon. That said, avoiding the marital-industrial complex didn't mean eschewing all drama. To that end, I brought home an order of spicy tuna rolls and a two-serving bottle of Veuve and asked that she come onto the roof with me. It meant climbing out the third-floor bedroom window onto the sloped—and possibly crumbling—shingles, a precarious place that she knew I had visited on numerous occasions.

She refused at first. I insisted, pointing out that while we were not the Jumbotron proposal type—I hate to make a scene in public—I didn't want to propose in just any old room of our house, either. We'd bought the downtown fixer-upper two years before, and while we loved its ramshackle charm, it wasn't what the moment called for. The roof, from this day forward, was for special occasions. As well, it was a pleasant autumn evening and there were plenty of stars on display. Sarah came around.

After we scrambled out and I positioned the blanket just so, I called her parents.

"Hi, Debbie, it's Ben calling. Can I speak to Jake?"

"Yes, just a minute."

Even this tradition is a tricky one, I thought. Debbie could have assented just as easily as Jake, especially since all parties would concede that this was a polite but unnecessary gesture. But then, if I *was* observing tradition as a matter of etiquette, what would be the point of doing so incorrectly? Clearly, the modern groom should ask both parents, so as not to endorse a sexist tradition. But what if the bride's parents are generous, warm and intelligent people who have a bad habit of using speakerphone?

"Hi, Ben. What's up?"

"Hi, Jake. I'm, uh, calling because I'd like to ask you a question."

"Of course. Go ahead."

Obviously, he knew. I paused to formulate the wording. I'd figured it would be best to put the request in my own words, to underline the fact that, though this was the respectful thing to do, I was doing it because I wanted to and not because the script said I should.

"I'm on the roof, and I'd like to ask for Sarah's hand in marriage."

Some things can't really be improved upon.

"Ben, you have our blessing. Why are you on the roof? Isn't that dangerous?"

I explained, and admitted that there was a modicum of danger involved. It was anticlimactic. I changed the subject, surprising all parties.

"I also want to tell you that I'm going to convert to Judaism. I've decided that it's important to raise our children in one religion, and I've been impressed by what I've seen of Judaism in your family. I think it's the right thing to do."

In that breath, I committed to having kids, a decision we'd never formally made. That night on the roof, I was making commitments as if they were going out of style. Now there was a pause on his end of the line.

"You know, you don't have to be Jewish to raise a Jewish family. It's a very nice gesture, though."

"I know. It's something I want to do."

And then I handed the phone to Sarah. She explained that we had no idea where the wedding might be, or when. She also admitted that the news of conversion was only somewhat expected. I then made the proposal proper, which didn't involve getting down on one knee—I might have slipped and fallen onto the barbecue three stories below—or even a ring—Debbie offered to sell me her mother's for a dollar. After Sarah formally accepted, we reclined side by side, looking at the stars and talking about religion, kids, marriage and the distinct possibility that one day we would need a new roof.

We came to this point—engaged and ready to commit and recommit to the original Abrahamic religion—via the Bronx.

That's where Sarah's grandmother Mildred Lempert was born, though I only met her seventy-three years later in Montreal, the city in which she had raised three daughters, outlived two husbands and settled on the more fitting name of Marsha Davis.

She was the kind of lady who drank screwdrivers, called you a doll and said that, after Ted and Murray, she just wanted a gay man to take her dancing. She'd have stage-whispered conversations with her granddaughter in front of me.

"You know what I say about your boyfriend, Sarah?"

"What do you say, bubby?"

"I say 'hubba hubba!'"

She also used the phrase "va-va-va-voom," which frankly doesn't get used enough. Her philosophy of life was simple, and she repeated it often: "You have to have a P.M.A.—Positive Mental Attitude!" Modern happiness research has validated her findings. Grandparenting is easier than parenting, or so the bumper stickers say, but Marsha made it seem as though parenting was just a warmup exercise.

"Sandy always used to tell me, 'Mom, cut to the point,'" Marsha once recalled. "But it's very hard for me to do! I somehow wind up talking and talking about all kinds of inconsequential details, and it's just not fun for someone else to have to hear them!"

"I enjoy it," I said, pandering only slightly. "Have you always been that way?"

"Yes, unless I catch myself, but even then! Even in writing! At least when I'm writing a letter, I can control it a bit. There are times when I learned to cut it short, but often I do ramble on."

Obviously, this was more fun for someone who had never heard her stories, but she didn't just want to dwell on the past. Though she'd lived in Montreal for fifty-seven years, Marsha was always impressed by the new restaurants the family would visit.

"I love when the girls take me around, because it feels like a city I've never seen," she'd say between bites of calamari at a Portuguese seafood restaurant. She was Jewish, of course, but her observance didn't extend to appetizers.

"I've never even seen some of these streets!

"It's nice to go browsing. I love to browse. I haven't browsed much, and there are parts of the city I still haven't seen."

Soon after we met, Marsha was diagnosed with lung cancer. She became less carefree and more absent-minded, and chemotherapy turned her blond bouffant into close-cropped grey curls.

One weekend long before our engagement, my mother invited Debbie and Marsha down to Vermont. There was no official occasion for the visit, though my mother is always looking for an opportunity to prepare a giant feast for unsuspecting visitors. Ever since my sister went off to school, my mother has lived alone in the Green Mountain State—though she would interject that she actually lives with Sadie, her excitable standard poodle, and Little Cat, her little cat. She works the evening shift as a nurse in a rehab centre, where she often makes dinner for the staff, and spends her days skiing, hiking or kayaking. She's been there since my parents divorced in 1992, and though she has plenty of friends and a busy life, she's become so used to her life alone that unfamiliar social situations bring on serious cases of nerves. That's my interpretation, of course. To dip into my little-used scientific education, I'm one of the variables in that equation: it could be that my presence puts my mom on edge. After the family schism, there was always low-level tension about what we expected of each other. Hosting Sarah's mother and grandmother was a wonderful, though not uncharacteristic, gesture, and I was especially happy to see my mother and Marsha take a quick liking to each other. We went to a teahouse in downtown Burlington, and at one point my mother was trying to remember the name of an old Montreal acquaintance. Marsha saw that she was deep in thought and reached over to pull an imaginary feather from my mother's imaginary hat.

"*Doink!*" she exclaimed.

We all froze for a second, then realized what her gesture meant. She was reaching into my mom's mind and fishing out the lost piece of information, a service performed without irony by a woman whose own memory was fading. It was a tiny bit sad, but mostly funny, and when we decided to view it as a joke at the expense of old age rather than one brought on by it, it became a defiant bit of physical comedy. I did it to Sarah for the rest of the afternoon, and my mother still does it to me.

In 2005, when it seemed as though the cancer was in remission, Debbie decided it was Marsha's last chance to visit her older brother Phil in Beverly Hills. For reasons I didn't think to question, Sarah and I were invited along for a week in sunny California. We jumped at the chance. It was the best sort of family vacation, partly because this wasn't my family and partly because, while Debbie drove the rental car and Sarah navigated the expressways, Marsha and I were the children in the back seat. She wore big, black, wraparound sunglasses and chatted happily about her childhood with her brother. I kept her reminiscing as best I could, and when she dozed off I took the opportunity to nap as well.

Phil and Rae lived in a tidy house in the shadow of the Flynt Publications building. He spoke like Marsha and wisecracked like her, too, and it made you feel profoundly unlucky not to have been born in the Bronx in the 1920s. Phil clearly realized this, as he'd typed out his childhood stories about stickball in the streets and read them aloud to us. "Look at that kid," Phil said, pointing to a baby picture of himself. "Head like a lemon."

Phil and Rae's three children lived in parts of SoCal as different as they were. The brainy lawyers on Manhattan Beach took us down to the boardwalk for a stroll, where we realized how pasty and emaciated visiting Canadians looked among the natives. On their San Diego patio, the interventional radiologist and his real-estate agent wife served us Champagne with a frozen strawberry in each glass ("It's my invention!" she said) and led us in a California toast, in which each person clinks glasses with the one beside them. The pediatric dentist to the stars was married to a sitcom writer, who explained in their Los Angeles home that the writing room on the new Chris Rock sitcom was purposely filled with schlubby white guys like him because comedy has to be universal. He also explained that he got his first meeting with a television executive by showing up with a box of Oreos.

I was happy to meet this cast of characters—again, they were not my family and I had no obligation but to enjoy their hospitality. My only request on the trip was a visit to the In-N-Out Burger. It was happily granted. The restaurant at Sunset and La Brea felt like the crossroads of southern California, with goths, ravers, preppies, seniors, immigrants, tourists and members of subcultures I could only guess at, all happily chewing their burgers together. We sat across from a Meryl Streep lookalike memorizing lines from *Ask the Dust*. I approached the counter and ordered four burgers. Marsha impressed everyone by finishing hers first, and we both went for seconds as well as paper hats.

We returned home. A year later, the cancer returned. It was neither slow nor quick, a pace that had the horrible effect of letting you see the moxie draining away before your eyes.

When she was first admitted to the long-term care facility in the Montreal suburb of Côte Saint-Luc, we came right away. We talked and joked and even got her to say a half-hearted "va-va-va-voom," but the positive mental attitude was hard to enforce.

We took the train back to Toronto that afternoon, knowing that we'd soon be returning to Marsha's bedside. As we sat on a train car filled with both sunlight and obnoxious teenagers, I found myself considering the sad reality of her future and the potential ours held.

"It's so difficult to see her like this, with tubes stuck in her," Sarah whispered. We hadn't been talking about it, but we each knew the other was thinking about it. Sarah's eyes were shiny but not teary. I tried to put scrambled thoughts into words and found they were unlike any I'd spoken before.

"It makes me think that, you know, if we were going to ever get married—or even if we weren't, but if we continue living together like we are now—now would be the time to say it."

"Oh, wow," Sarah said. "Well, of course."

"It's a big, dramatic gesture, I know—maybe a bit melo-dramatic—but this is a big, dramatic moment, right?"

"It is."

"And it would give her something—give everyone some-thing—happy to think about."

"It would."

"And I know this isn't expected of me—actually, it'll be completely unexpected—but I think I want to convert to Juda-ism, too."

"What?"

What, indeed. Also, why? Soon to be followed by where? And how? At least we knew I was the who and now was the when.

I couldn't really explain the impulse. It was still an idea at this point, one I thought I'd try vocalizing on the 5 p.m. express train just to see if I was serious.

"I admit it's not something I've thought a lot about, but whenever I have thought about it, it seemed like the right thing to do. And I don't mean like, morally right or whatever. I want to join your family, so that in situations like this I can be counted on and relied upon. Obviously, I can do that as a gentile, but I think there's still a barrier there—I don't know the traditions, the customs, the history. Learning the religion—joining it—would show everyone how serious I was. When I've seen the way your family comes together at times like this, Juda-ism seems like a great comfort. I see the consolation it gives your mother. More than that, it tells them what to do and how to do it. When my family is in similar situations, they sort of make it up as they go along. That really drains the ceremony out of life's important moments. And our wedding will be one of life's big moments. I don't want to make it up as we go, making up cheesy vows and not giving it the respect and ceremony it deserves. I want to do it our way, but I also want to do it the right way."

I was serious, I realized. And when I told Sarah's parents three days later, it was official. We returned to Montreal shortly thereafter for Marsha's final days. Her three daughters were at her bedside around the clock, giving her water with a sponge and holding her hand. She could not speak, but could manage a slight smile with eyes half open. That was how she greeted our news.

Spreading the Good Word

I was now officially an aspiring Jew, a condition I'd assumed before really considering what it meant. The first stumbling block, I realized, was that I had very little idea why I was pursuing this course. If the point was to have something in common with Sarah's family, I could have nurtured a love of Balkan dance. Instead, I'd made a public commitment to joining a religion I didn't know much about. I allowed myself to consider the possibility that this was a mistake.

Marsha's funeral convinced me otherwise, at least temporarily. My previous brushes with death had begun to establish a pattern, one that only became clear on this occasion. When my grandfather and uncle, both on my father's side, died within a year of each other, both funerals were sad in expected— and unexpected—ways. I expected to see my father tear up during the powerful eulogies he delivered at both, and to see my grandmother looking frail and shaken by the loss of her husband and son. I didn't anticipate the tinny CD accompaniment of "Amazing Grace" or the lack of oxygen in the small-town funeral parlour.

The Erretts gathered together uncomfortably. Though there was plenty of Kleenex on offer, the tears were limited. Here, I realized, was where the consolations of religion would come in handy. Even if you don't believe a priest has a special relationship with God, he would know how to provide the counsel and comfort a memorial service ought to feature. The Erretts would still be a reserved family of Anglo-Canadian Protestants, but there seemed no discernible benefit to not having religion at times like these.

Though the Jewish funerals I had been to seemed odd at the time, the presence of traditions, even unfamiliar ones, was a definite improvement. The first was for my friend Jon's mother, who died when we were both in university. It was the first time I had worn a kippah. I remember being surprised and faintly embarrassed when the cantor began to sing in the middle of the service. The Hebrew prayer he intoned sounded like a wail of despair. I looked around to see tears streaming down cheeks and realized I was tearing up, too.

The next was for Helena, Sarah's paternal grandmother. I didn't know her very well, but the lack of Lazarovic males helped elevate me to the status of pallbearer. It was then I learned that Jews consider it a duty and an honour to help bury the dead, which meant that after the funeral attendees witnessed the lowering of the coffin into the ground, each mourner was to take the shovel and participate in the burial. This, I realized, was closure, something the airless funeral parlour could not offer.

I was a pallbearer once again at Marsha's funeral. This time I felt I knew the deceased well enough to be worthy of the position. The service had all the cathartic rituals I'd experienced before, and this time I was a larger part of them. This was also my first real experience of sitting shiva. The word, Sarah told me, meant seven. For seven days after the burial, the family mourns together. Friends visit with food, help with chores and share stories about the deceased. This again struck me as an ideal, a community response to mortality. I considered how difficult it must have been for my grandmother to return to her empty house after two funerals.

Immediately after Marsha's funeral, there was a reception at Ruby Foo's, a once-great Chinese restaurant on Montreal's Décarie Expressway that had devolved into a crumbling hotel frequented by nostalgic expats. It was there that we began the strange process of spreading the news of our engagement and my conversion to the assembled mourners.

"It's such a mitzvah that you're doing this now," Miscellaneous Distant Cousin #2 said.

"We just wanted to tell Marsha some good news," Sarah replied.

"And soon, I'll know what a mitzvah is," I added. "I mean, beyond knowing that they come after bars."

"So it's true that you're converting!"

"Well, he doesn't have to!" Sarah disclaimed. "It was his idea!"

This was the start of Sarah's discomfort with the idea, something that hadn't come up in our train or rooftop chats. After our inquisitors had left for the buffet, I asked her about it.

"What did that mean, that it was my idea?"

"Well, it was, right? I just don't want them to think I forced you into it."

"Oh." I paused, having not previously considered this interpretation of events. "Would they think that? It makes it sound like you don't want any part of it. One of the reasons I said I'd do it was to bring us closer."

"I know that, but other people might not, is all. It's not like you've talked about it before. For them, it came out of the blue."

"I guess so. Well, I'd be more emphatic that it was *my* decision, but I can barely explain my motivation to you, let alone to some cousin I don't know."

"You can still back out of it, you know. Everyone would understand."

"Is that what you want? I thought it was the right thing to do."

"You're making me sound ungrateful, like a self-hating Jew. Of course I'm happy you're doing it, it's just . . . a lot to process right now."

I hugged Sarah. This wasn't a fight, exactly; neither of us was upset. It was more a state of confusion, the result of making a big gesture without really considering what came next. We were emotionally befuddled when two of Sarah's second cousins approached us with congratulations on our engagement.

"*Mazel tov!*" Tamara said, giving Sarah a hug. She turned her gaze to me and demanded, "You're not really going to convert, are you?"

"Well, yes, I am," I responded.

"I think that's a bad idea," Tamara said with a half-smile.

"Why would you want to become Jewish? Are you aware that it's not a very popular religion? You know, through history. Unless you go in for pogroms."

This was a thought I'd refused to acknowledge. As a heterosexual, white, vaguely Christian male, I'd never faced discrimination of any sort. I hadn't had strong opinions on the Middle East, other than that they should all just knock it off. Reports of hate crimes had distressed me, but they all seemed equally reprehensible. All of these thoughts came swirling into my head at once. I pushed them aside to concentrate on the inquisition at hand.

"You know, Jewish law commands us to formally discourage your plans to convert," Deborah, the other second cousin, explained, also with half a smile. There was a full smile between them, but I couldn't quite add it up.

"Seriously, though, why would you go through with that? For the food? You know, anyone can eat bagels these days," Tamara said.

"Um, I just think it's the right thing to do . . . for a number of reasons . . . all of which are complicated," I said. Sarah, momentarily thrown off by our previous conversation, finally took pity upon me.

"He just wants to join the family," Sarah said. "To be *mish-pachah*."

"I first want to know what *mish* . . . uh, that word means."

"And that's really the point," Sarah told her cousins, who seemed satisfied with the answer. We made a break for the buffet, where my mother was picking at the lox. She had driven up from Vermont for the funeral but, in keeping with a record of unpunctuality reinforced throughout my childhood—most memorably when I was the last kid to be picked up from track practice for the entire season—missed the service proper and came straight to the cemetery for the interment. I was just relieved that she made it. Disregarding her tardiness—it is an unavoidable genetic trait, I tell Sarah every time I keep her waiting—she was making a kind gesture toward my future in-laws, one informed by her own unfortunate history of families by marriage who never got along in the best of times and helped make the worst of rocky ones. Despite her anxiety at being surrounded by unfamiliar people, she was here to back me up. On the subject of conversion, she was even willing to lead the charge. "I think it's a wonderful thing you're doing, son," she said to me. "If it will help, I can convert, too."

"I don't think that's necessary, but I appreciate it."

"What will you have to do? Are there classes?"

"I don't really know."

"I guess it's good that we gave you an Old Testament name. And that we had you circumcised."

"Uh, yeah," I responded. I had officially begun to recognize that I knew very little about Judaism. At that moment, I also understood that friends, family and casual acquaintances would feel at liberty to ask and joke about my genitals. I would need some snappy comebacks. These were particularly necessary around the water cooler, where a Jewish colleague I'd never actually had a conversation with had somehow heard the news and wanted to welcome me to the tribe. "So, I hear you're going to join the chosen! *Mazel tov*!"

"Uh, thank you."

"When's the bris?"

"Sorry?"

"You know, the circumcision. You *do* know about that, right?"

"Of course! And I'm very glad my parents took care of all the surgical requirements early on."

"That's good. But don't you still have to have a drop of blood drawn?"

"Uh, I'm not sure about that."

"Yeah, the rabbi has to poke you down there. For ceremony, you know. Though I've heard some will let you draw a drop of blood from your index finger."

"Right, the index finger. That's the way I'm doing it. Just like that."

I didn't know how any of it was supposed to be done, though I did know most people's reference points were either the "yada yada" episode of *Seinfeld* (in which Tim the dentist converts for the jokes) or *Sex and the City* (in which Charlotte completes her conversion, visits the ceremonial bath and remains fabulous). Personally, my cultural touchstone was *The Big Lebowski*, which taught me, not incorrectly, that conversion was not something you undertook lightly. It was an eternal commitment, as Walter Sobchak, the burly Vietnam vet played by John Goodman, makes clear. When Walter's friends give him a hard time for observing his ex-wife's religion despite being born Polish Catholic, he screams, "What do you think happens when you get divorced? You turn in your library card? Get a new driver's licence? Stop being Jewish?"

Walter also brandished a firearm during league play and refused to bowl on the Sabbath, neither of which was of immediate help to me. For the month after the engagement and Marsha's funeral, conversations inevitably ended with me admitting I had no idea what came next. The proposal had been public and my intentions clear; now it was time to put aside the metaphysical considerations and figure out how to do it, if in fact I really was going to do it. At this point, I didn't know that the word "Israel" directly translates as "he who wrestles with God," but I knew I was ready to don my cape, tights and yarmulke and jump into the ring.

Location, Location, Location

You would think that finding a place to worship—an organization you would be part of for the rest of your life, one that would help you raise your children and mourn your parents—would be considerably more difficult than finding a place to have your wedding, where you would eat a mediocre dinner and watch your new in-laws dance the hora. You would think that, but you would be wrong.

At this stage, in the colder part of the fall of 2006, Marsha's shiva had ended and our engagement became the focus of familial attention. Debbie, emotionally drained by her mother's long illness—and the long sift through the decades of flea-market acquisitions Marsha had crammed into her Montreal apartment—was ready to start the wedding planning. Which was fine by us: Sarah had no intention of reading bridal magazines, and I insisted that our wedding be low-key and stress-free—though I also wanted top-notch food and a huge dance party for all our friends. The self-delusion was there from the beginning.

Where did we want to do the deed? Toronto was the obvious choice, one that would depend on the synagogue we joined. Having attended one too many weddings at which the potentially inebriated guests were expected to drive from venue to venue, we knew we wanted the ceremony and reception to be held in one place, but where? I realized that, with all the invitations I received through work, I had seen many of the city's potential event venues up close. And I knew that, barring any professional misfortunes, I'd likely be seeing them again after the wedding. I had a vision of attending a dull corporate event in what was once our wedding hall, pointing out to a colleague that it was right over there, where that sad chocolate fountain was sputtering away, that Sarah and I exchanged vows. In this vision, I then reminded the colleague in question that the reason chocolate fountains flow so readily is that half of the chocolate is vegetable oil. This image didn't help matters.

"What about getting married in Florida?" Sarah asked. "We could do it in January, so all our friends would get a nice vacation. Plus, if my mom's going to do all the work anyway, it might as well be convenient for her."

A wedding in the land of manatees and senior citizens sounded too kitschy at first, but then I realized it could solve my chocolate fountain dilemma. I was worried about picking a lame locale at home, but picking one in the sunshiney land of chintz would be like doubling down. Our friends would thank us for the excuse to escape a salt-stained Canadian winter. We could be married on the beach by a barefoot rabbi, have a kosher luau afterward and the next day's breakfast at Waffle House. It was ridiculous, and thus perfect.

"I like it!" I told Sarah, who told her mother in Boca Raton, who in turn began her planning. When we went down over the holidays, she'd take us to some potential locales and we'd get everything squared away. In the meantime, Sarah began to investigate the conversion process. All this out-sourcing was terrific.

To become a Jew, Sarah found, I needed to take a year of classes. To enrol, I needed a sponsoring rabbi. That entailed consulting with Sarah's extended family, followed by plenty of time on the telephone. We agreed that Sarah would handle this. Her job as a freelance illustrator and filmmaker meant she worked from home, so there were no cubicle-mates to listen to her conversations. More importantly, there was no danger of her accidentally asking what time Mass was held. (This was only the beginning of my uncertainty about language. I wasn't about to call any of the rabbis "Father," but was their speech called a sermon? Are shul members called a congregation? Each of these words seemed like a carefully baited linguistic trap. I did soon learn that a shul is a synagogue, and both can be referred to as temples, though not all Jews are onside with this: some believe the only temple was the first one, built in Jerusalem.)

Like most North American Jews, Sarah's family is Reform. From what I could figure out, that meant you didn't have to be kosher and certainly didn't need the black hats, ringlets, skullcaps and all the other accessories you'd see people wearing in devout parts of town. That was Orthodox Judaism, and somewhere between the two was Conservative Judaism. Further afield were more hippy-dippy flavours of the faith, which seemed to involve a lot of guitar playing, mysticism and celebrities.

Our first prospect for a religious home was one of the largest temples in the city, the one frequented by all the downtown Jews we knew. (Do you "frequent" temple? In practice few do, but grammatically?) Sarah called to arrange a visit, but was told that they'd already met their quota. This seemed like a bad joke: How are righteous converts like parking tickets? I suppose you need a certain percentage of the congregation (congregation? Yes, this was correct) knowing what to do to avoid a chaotic service, but still, given the concerns about declining populations of Jewry, this seemed odd. Unless, of course, it was another one of those attempts to dissuade potential converts.

Our next option was a similarly large Reform synagogue found at the end of a long bus ride. We scheduled our visit before work one day, and as we sat on the bus for forty-five minutes, I tried to rationalize the weekly commute.

"If I came straight from work, it would only be a twenty-dollar cab ride."

"But I'd still have to take this bus, and then we'd need to take it home," Sarah replied. "There go our Friday nights."

"Well, what if we went on Saturday? We could rent an AutoShare car."

"But we'd be on the clock while we were in temple. It would cost us ten dollars an hour to be good Jews."

"That's minimum wage," I replied, realizing that that didn't advance either side of the argument. "And while we're up here, we could go to Costco."

"Do we really want to go to Costco every week? Shabbat is supposed to be a day of rest, and watching fat people shove samples of trail mix down their throats is not my idea of rest."

She had a point—a fattist point that overlooked the tremendous value to be found at my favourite suburban big-box outlet, but a point nonetheless.

When we arrived, we had to pass a security guard to get in. I'd never done this at a house of worship, and found it a bit unsettling. I'd seen the odd story on hate crimes and read about the occasional vandalized tombstone, but was this really necessary? Notwithstanding my impression that I could overpower this not-particularly-threatening rent-a-cop, I thought these sorts of measures were, in part, self-fulfilling prophecies. If people see a guard, they assume something needs to be guarded, and fear begets suspicion, closed doors and other bad things. Of course, if it were my grandfather's grave that had been spray-painted, I might not be so lovey-dovey. At any rate, I knew I didn't want to pass through security each week if I could avoid it.

The rabbi was a pleasant woman who asked Sarah a series of questions I didn't think she'd be able to answer. Lo and behold, she knew her Jewish rituals. This was the first time since the walking tour that I'd seen that long-lost knowledge deployed, and it remained impressive.

Then it was my turn. I summarized the story of our engagement and added the touching coda about wanting to raise our children in a shared faith. I didn't want to dwell on our theoretical children when talking with family members, but figured it would be a good three-for-the-price-of-two selling point for a congregation. Then came the circumcision question, asked officially for the first time. The teasing questions had prepared me for it; I assured her that had been taken care of early on and noted how thankful I was for my parents' foresightedness about foreskins. It was comforting that she seemed as relieved about that as I was. We were feeling pretty good about the interview, at least until we exited the synagogue and found ourselves once more in the middle of nowhere. This wasn't going to work.

Next, we set out to investigate a small shul just a few blocks from our house. The thought of walking to temple from our house and meeting friends for dinner at a nearby restaurant afterward made sense to us. "When I'm done worshipping, I'd rather be near a French bistro than a big-box store," Sarah reasoned as we walked over. I couldn't argue with her logic.

In religion as in real estate, the three most important considerations are location, location and location—and frankly, the old realtor's trick of baking a pie before an open house would work just as well with synagogues. This temple didn't do that, though it had a number of other advantages. First, it was tiny. The warehouses of worship we had seen before reminded me of those megachurches in the southern U.S. that contain their own Starbucks, malls, daycares and functioning ecosystems in case of Rapture. This was a small building on a residential street of Victorian houses. It was the difference between seeing a band at a small bar or at a stadium, only the band in question was God.

The small physical space—wooden pews, non-stained-glass windows, elegant wooden dais at the front—was also only used three times a week: on Friday to welcome the Sabbath, on Saturday morning for bar mitzvahs and a Sabbath service, and on Sunday morning to begin the week anew. As I was already looking for reasons to choose this religious home base, I decided to view this as a big advantage. If, I reasoned, something in the conversion process flipped a switch in my mind and turned me superdevout, I'd only be here on the weekends. I realized this wasn't a rationale to share with the rabbi.

The second selling point was the lack of a guard at the door. The fact that we were in a peaceful neighbourhood, inhabited primarily by university professors and students, likely helped on this count. As well, there was a Save Darfur placard on the lawn, where at other synagogues there were only United Jewish Appeal fundraising placards. Obviously, it's important to support your community at its house of assembly, but I liked the reminder that being a part of this community made you a part of the world at large.

And then we met the rabbi. I remember thinking the process was like dating—we thought it would be a good match, but who knows if we'd really hit it off. To uncomfortably extend the dating metaphor, this was the person I'd have to strip down before for the ceremonial bath, if the *Sex and the City* recaps I'd been privy to were to be believed. And then there was the whole idea of a spiritual elder: great in theory, but would we really want to tell this guy our problems? And how do you break it to a man of faith that you're not really sure you have that much to begin with?

"Ben and Sarah? Right! Come on in and have a seat!"

He wore his skullcap—"*Kippah*," Sarah corrected. "It sounds less medical in Hebrew"—with a suit and a warm smile. If the rabbi we'd met in the 'burbs had a bit of the soccer mom about her, this rabbi fit his surroundings just as well: trim, scholarly and articulate, he could have passed for a professor at the nearby university. His office seemed to double as the synagogue's common room, library and administrative offices.

"Welcome to our shul. Why don't you tell me a bit about yourselves?" Sarah led off, dazzling me once again with her command of Hebrew. I'm not sure the rabbi was as taken aback. I told the grandmother story again, adding new details to keep it fresh for Sarah.

"Why don't you tell me a bit about your religious background?" he asked, and since I had a good feeling about the place, I decided to push the envelope a bit.

"Well, I was raised Catholic, but to be honest I never really got it. We only went to Mass on Christmas and Easter and when we visited my grandmother, but nothing about the experience really convinced me that, uh, there was a God. I mean, I'm willing to believe in something, but I don't know what shape that belief takes."

"You should know that there is no test of faith in Judaism. In fact, you can be a good Jew and not believe in God. Judaism is about what you do and how you live your life. We have members who don't believe in God and are quite open about it. The important part is to act in a way that's consistent with Jewish teachings."

I was amazed to hear this. These were the doubts I was anxiously preparing to have but hadn't quite formulated yet, and here was this man of God, shrugging them off within five minutes of our introduction.

"Wow," I said. "I'm certainly willing to do that. We've

liked what we've seen so far, and I think we'd like to join this shul." My enthusiasm was obvious, possibly too much so.

"Well, it's important that you try out services at different synagogues. They're very different, and it depends where you feel most comfortable. Although I'm a Reform rabbi, this is an egalitarian Conservative shul. That means services are in Hebrew, though I give sermons in English. And because we're a small shul, we don't have a cantor."

"How small is small?" I asked.

"About six hundred congregants. The bigger synagogues in the city have about ten times that number."

"How do they all fit?"

"Well, they don't, which is why we use the gymnasium at the Jewish Community Centre on the High Holidays."

The thought of sitting through a religious service in a gym made me think of assemblies in junior high at which I would pass the time by counting light fixtures. I resolved not to do that.

"How does it work with attendance every week?" I asked.

"We don't take it," he smiled.

"I guess what I mean to say is, uh, do people come every week?"

"We get a pretty full house on Saturday morning, especially for bar mitzvahs. There's a dedicated group here on Fridays to welcome Shabbat. Sunday mornings, it's sometimes difficult to get a *minyan*"—he saw my blank look—"that's the ten Jews you need to daven together, or pray." As I was committed to entering into this religion of my own free will and on my own terms, I decided to ask the question I was thinking.

"Are members expected to show up every week?"

"Well, it can't hoyt," he smiled. Sarah laughed at his odd Bugs Bunny–esque New Yorkese pronunciation. That convinced me this was the place. We made plans to attend services.

Sitting in temple that weekend, I realized that perhaps I'd built it up too much. The rabbi was a cool guy, but this was still a religious function. In form, it wasn't much different from what I'd sat through as a bored child. As an adult, though, I was able to keep from studying the ceiling. If I'd been asked to draw up a program, it would look like this:

✡ Holy man in front reads from book; congregants follow along silently and all say "Amen" together.

✡ Holy man gives new page number; congregants read along out loud.

✡ A song or two is sung.

✡ Everyone stands for a prayer, then sits down again.

✡ A prayer for the bereaved is said.

✡ The sermon is delivered. Current events are acknowledged and tied into religious texts.

✡ Wine is sipped.

✡ There is more reading.

✡ Another song is sung.

✡ Stand for another prayer.

✡ Announcements from the bulletin are made.

✡ Final song is sung.

✡ Acknowledge other congregants on the way out.

Which pretty well describes every religious service I've ever been to, which makes you wonder why interfaith harmony is so hard to achieve. Missing, of course, was the bite to eat my father called communion, though there apparently was a kiddush snack served in the basement after Saturday service.

Of course, there was the language barrier. At first, this seemed like a bad thing: I had no idea what everyone was saying. It really made me feel like an outsider, especially when I looked over at Sarah and saw that she knew all the words.

"I had no idea what was going on in there!" I whined to her after we were out of shul-shot.

"You could follow along, though, right? It's your first time ever. What did you expect?"

"Well, I expected some of the songs to have a tune, at least."

"They totally have a tune. You just don't know them. And maybe it's better not to sing in English, anyway."

"Why wouldn't we want to know what we were singing?"

"Some of the prayers are pretty Biblical, if you know what I mean. People are smited, God is angry, we praise him, we beg forgiveness, and so on."

Though I honestly didn't hear the tunes, even my Christian ears couldn't miss the prayer known as the Shema. It's sung by the whole congregation and sounds like this: "*Shema Yisrael Adonai Eloheinu Adonai Ehad.*"

It is oddly haunting and beautiful; the "nai" in *Adonai* is drawn out until the rabbi's voice wavers ever so slightly, and it gives you this weird chill that must be an evolutionary response to prayer. It didn't make me a believer—not that I even had to be—but it made me pay attention for that moment. Our prayer books had the English translations on the facing pages, and this one was: "Hear, O Israel! The Lord is our God! The Lord is One!"

Which didn't make sense until Sarah told me that, in addition to being a headline-making country in the Middle East, Israel could also refer to all the Jews. Even then, though, there was the God part, which seemed like a statement of the obvious. Sarah reminded me that back in the days of paganism, this wasn't necessarily the case.

She also pointed out that having everyone sing along, while at first isolating for those of us who didn't know the words, was actually the ideal situation. Sarah had many memories of the Broadway-style cantor at her childhood temple, stealing the show with Mariah Carey–like vocal stylings, in effect turning the attention of the congregation away from the big man upstairs and toward her heavenly voice. When we attended a service at one of the bigger temples, I saw what she meant: it was as if you were at a concert, albeit the sort of concert you'd never, ever attend. At our temple, there was no danger of diva-ism. The raspy old men sang just as loudly as the tone-deaf teenagers, and while the result might not have had harmony, it was certainly spirited.

We saw the rabbi after the service, and I decided to continue my campaign of candour.

"Sarah, Ben, *shabbat shalom*. How was the service?"

"Well, rabbi, to be honest I didn't get very much of it."

"That's understandable. It can be a bit intimidating at first. Remember, the more you put in, the more you'll get out of it."

We waited a week to make it clear we'd given the matter the proper amount of thought, during which time we received the first email bulletin from the temple. In it we learned the following:

✡ The shul ran a regular outreach program to a nearby nursing home, so their elderly Jews could observe the Sabbath.

✡ The annual Hanukkah party was just around the corner, and there was still time to be in the rollicking skit.

✡ Jewish Charity Salsa Classes are much more than dance lessons! For one thing, the money goes to charity. For another, it's Jewish Salsa dancing!

✡ The Miss Judea contest held in Poland in 1929 attracted more than a hundred entrants and marked an important moment in interwar Zionism, according to an upcoming lecture.

✡ Yaakov's daughter Dinah was raped in this week's Torah reading, and in response her brothers killed everyone in the aggressor's city. Was this justified? Commentators debated both points, with Maimonides arguing that because the offending tribe had failed to hold one of their own to account, they were all guilty. Nachmanides, on the other hand, points out that they broke a number of God's laws, none of which made slaughter okay. The rabbi used this reading to touch on modern justice. Instead of answers, he offered up questions: "How severe should we be in using the instruments of law to punish offenders? How merciful should we be in the application of the law, in the hope that offenders will repent? That a horrific crime was committed against Dinah is not in doubt. How to respond in a way that meets the needs of the victim, and society at large, is much less clear."

✡ The potluck was coming up.

I was impressed by the food, charity and opportunity to salsa dance my new religion afforded, but mostly I was impressed by the Torah thought. I'd never heard this story before, but it sounded like what I knew of what Christians call the Old Testament: people are slaughtered, vengeance is sought, more people are killed, and that's that. The fact that the grisly parts weren't glossed over and that there was no definite conclusion—let alone the one-size-fits-all "And that's why God loves us all so much"—was strangely refreshing. No faith and no easy answers sounded more like graduate school than religion. I saw this as a definite asset. And if God's children could bust a few Latin moves on the dance floor while they mulled over the puzzle, so much the better.

I emailed our rabbi and confirmed that we were ready to join the shul. We liked the building, the people, the vibe, the newsletter and the man in charge. He agreed to be our sponsoring rabbi, and Sarah enrolled us in the Jewish Information Classes beginning in early January. Though it was only November and we hadn't even set a wedding date—at the very soonest, assuming the class went well and everything else came together, it was fourteen months away—we were ready for our tour of Floridian wedding venues.

✡ ✡ ✡

The first thing you notice when you deplane at Fort Lauderdale–Hollywood International Airport is the air. It's humid, with a tang of salt water and jet fuel, which for me summons everything that is Florida. The second thing you notice is all the plastic surgery. Those young people embracing their grandchildren at the arrivals gate appear to be happy, but why aren't they smiling? Oh, right—Botox. You remember that no one's age or emotional state can be read on their faces, or any other body part, for that matter.

I love this ridiculousness of the Sunshine State, though I wouldn't want to live with it full time. For much of my young life, my grandmother Laurette had the right idea, staying down south just long enough to miss the Canadian winter without forfeiting her Canadian health care.

This year's trip was my fourth annual, so there would be no surprises. (Well, one: Debbie's gift of Judaica in the form of a silver kiddush cup. I disguised my befuddlement with gratitude.) When the Lazarovic girls came home, the agenda was purposely kept sparse. They were expected to consolidate two boxes of childhood memorabilia into one. Jake would take us to his favourite new restaurants in the neighbourhood. I would present my future father-in-law with a bottle of duty-free Scotch, which we would make a small dent in over the course of the week. I would make a point of using the pool every day, leading to a daily observation from Debbie that they never use it because it's just too cold. Sarah would agonize over seeing old friends, and we'd end up visiting only a quarter of those she'd contacted. If the Jewish calendar permitted it, we would be the guests of honour at the annual Lazarovic Hanukkah party, which featured Debbie's carrot and potato latkes and a traditional family jam session—Sarah on squeaky violin, Jake on drums, Debbie on one of the many exotic instruments she used to teach her preschool music class, Becky, if she was around, on clarinet, Jane, the littlest Lazarovic, on the double bass she studied, and me desperately trying to stay on beat with a tambourine. I realize it sounds like a family-that-plays-together-stays-together tableau, but that's how it is.

This year, Jane was down from Montreal, where she had just finished her music degree at McGill. (She had wisely followed Becky's northward trajectory.) Seven years younger than Sarah, she shared her wild blond hair and father's nose, but enjoyed the advantage of being the less-monitored youngest child. Her teenage days were spent as the only child still in Florida, while her teenage nights were spent doing all manner of off-the-record things at South Florida raves. She'd put her musicality to good use in challenging her father's authority, most memorably in her oft-intoned mock-spiritual *"He woke me at seven-thirty / Just to show me some crumbs."* This dated back to a late night out followed by a before-bed snack in the kitchen, the remnants of which Jake found the next morning. Jane had expertly turned his means of discipline into a very catchy song, one her father had to endure many years after said crumbs were swept away. Not that he really seemed to mind, so happy was he to have his girls home.

Jane accompanied Debbie, Sarah and me on our tour of South Florida wedding locales, a day-long jaunt that was intended to give us an idea of what was out there. I pictured a slightly ramshackle motel on the beach with a name like Boca Breezes. I soon realized that (a) there was no such place; (b) if there *were* such a place, it was the last place Jake would want to have the wedding; (c) by outsourcing the wedding planning—and presumably a good chunk of the tab, though we hadn't had that talk yet—we were forfeiting some of our control over the particulars. I mentioned this to Sarah as we piled into Debbie's car for our day-long tour. Sarah had independently arrived at the same conclusion, but pointed out that we were here and appointments had been made, so buckle up.

Our first stop was a glassy tower overlooking a marina. We met up with a professional concierge who appeared to be exclusively in charge of shepherding eager couples around. "Congratulations!" she cooed in a most disingenuous way. I couldn't read the expression on her lifted face. "Let me see the ring!"

"It's actually my grandmother's," Sarah said, to my ears an explanation for its modest size.

"Oh, that's so lovely," our hostess said without betraying emotion. "Now let me walk you through the reception area!"

Debbie and Jane walked ahead while Sarah and I hung back. "I don't like this place at all," I whispered to her as we pretended to examine the floor-to-ceiling mirrors."

"This is classic Florida," Sarah said. "You said you wanted cheesy."

"Yeah, but I meant manatee cheesy, not Botox cheesy." Sarah hushed me, under the mistaken impression—as usual—that my whispers could be heard by everyone around us.

Our next stop was an Embassy Suites by the ocean. The space was marginally better, though we were distracted somewhat by Jane's remembrances of her youthful adventures.

"I haven't been in here since high school, when my pals and I used to come to eat a free breakfast."

"They gave you free breakfasts?" I asked, my reflexes dulled by Floridian opulence.

"Well, free breakfast for guests. We'd sneak in through the patio and help ourselves to the buffet. Eggs, French toast, bacon—you know. And the hash browns! So crispy and salty!"

"Didn't you eat at home?"

"Oh sure, but this was so good. At home, we'd have healthy breakfast cookies with no-fat margarine. This was our *real* breakfast. We were growing teens!"

"Didn't you get caught?" Sarah asked, perhaps worried in retrospect.

"We'd just make up a room number and when they went to check it, we'd leave. Eventually they figured us out and closed off the patio."

For fear of Jane being locked up—and the hotel's general dinginess; there was one of those overpatterned carpets that's meant to hide stains but actually accentuates them—we crossed that one off the list.

Jake met us for the last venue, a beachside hotel and private club that would have played host to Jay Gatsby back in the day. After a valet took the car, we wandered in to the marble-clad lobby and waited for the special weddings assistant. This was a level above our first stop, both in manners—no mention was made of the ring—and in complimentary beverages, I thought as I sipped limeade from a frosted glass. The vaulted ceilings, lush furnishings and gorgeous views were idyllic, and when we walked down the palm-lined foyer into the great hall, with its view of the ocean, I was gobsmacked.

"Could we do both the ceremony and the reception in this room?" I asked our guide. "Of course, sir. It's not a problem to move all the chairs out while your guests are dining."

As he led the Lazarovics through the hall, I sat on one of the many plush white armchairs and leafed through the information packets. My stack of thick cream-coloured paper included a price list, and the first number that jumped off the page was a chair-moving fee of $1,000. I nearly spat out my limeade. I had planned to maintain a don't-ask-don't-tell attitude on costs, but this was clearly ridiculous. I considered volunteering to move the chairs myself, but I'd likely have other things to do on my wedding day.

"That was very nice," I said once the valet had returned the car and we were safely on the road. "Maybe a bit much, though."

"A bit?" Sarah said. "I don't think it makes much sense to have our wedding at a hotel that none of our friends could afford to stay at."

"Well, I'm sure some of them could get a good rate at a cheaper hotel nearby," Debbie said.

"Or some of them could be chair movers for the weekend. It pays pretty well," I joked.

"This is the best of what Boca has to offer, guys," Jake said from behind his extra-thick prescription sunglasses.

"Maybe we should look farther afield," Sarah said.

"Maybe we should think about dinner," I said.

"I think my brother-fiancé has the right idea," Jane said. For the first time that day, we had consensus.

First Day of School

Who converts to Judaism? Lawyers, mostly. This was what we learned on the first night of Jew class. We weren't sure what to expect, as it had taken quite a few group emails to establish exactly when and where the classes would start, a process that had culminated in this message from a prospective classmate:

> Dear Everyone:
> Whoever is responsible for these emails, thank you so much.
> For me, I have decided to go to the Conservative
> Conversion classes and will not be attending the
> one thru the reform movement, so you can take me
> off your list.
> I want to wish everyone the very best in this exciting
> journey that we are (will be) taking and many hours of
> fruitful study. Be Well everyone.

The "many hours of fruitful study" bit scared me; I didn't think I'd ever used a term like that in a non-ironic context. Was this the sort of keener we'd be surrounded by? Or had they all been wooed away by the more disciplined environs of the Conservative program?

We received an information packet prior to the first night that promised that "an interesting and exciting programme has been planned for you, and we are looking forward to an exciting year." For thirty weeks, with a generous summer holiday, we would meet in a midtown elementary school classroom for rigorous study. The goal, however, was not to convert; this was a Jewish Information Class. I suppose the distinction was made so as not to disappoint those who didn't make it, but were there masochists who would partake in this purely for their own edification? It seemed unlikely. The information packet detailed five components of the course:

1. *Hebrew.* If you can't read it, you can't pray in it, so
   the goal was to become proficient by year's end.
2. *Synagogue Membership and Attendance.* "It is expected
   that candidates for conversion will attend Shabbat and
   holiday worship services regularly." In other words, you
   can't win if you don't pray.
3. *Weekly Classes.* Do your homework, etc.
4. *Shabbat Dinner.* At some point in the year, a dinner on
   the Sabbath would be held at the home of one of the
   teachers. Attendance wasn't mandatory.
5. *Class Attendance.* As that noted Talmudic scholar Woody
   Allen said, 80 percent of life is just showing up. This

applied to my better 50 percent, too. No matter how obvious the course material or simple the Hebrew lesson, she and I had the same obligation to be there.

This is where the stated goal of Jewish Information Class and the actual goal of conversion didn't quite jibe, but no one seemed to mind. As the course pack stated in bold italics: *You have assumed no obligation to convert to Judaism by joining this course, nor have the rabbis of the Beit Din assumed any obligation to accept you as a convert.* The class was simply a "testing ground for your motivations and feelings." If this passage was highlighted to prevent underqualified candidates from being disappointed, the point was really driven home by a warning farther down the page: *Please do not arrange for circumcision or Hatafat Dam Brit without consulting your sponsoring rabbi.* Yikes.

I had to take a taxi from work to arrive on time, a twenty-five-dollar weekly cost I decided to view as another test of my devotion. I met Sarah at the temple door and we checked in with security.

"So this is where we'll be, every Tuesday until you're a Jew," Sarah said as we waited for the elevator. "That sounds like a folksy expression. 'We'll be here every Tuesday until the cows come home or until you're a Jew, whichever comes first.' But don't forget that education is a journey, not a destination. Especially for Jews."

"I feel like every sentence could end with 'especially for Jews.'"

"How about: 'It's a shame to miss concerts or parties that

happen on Tuesdays. Especially for Jews.'" We didn't usually trade quips at such speed, but we were nervous, and screwball comedy became our coping mechanism.

We passed the children's art in the hallway, chose kid-sized seats in the classroom and stole glances at our fellow students. They all looked about our age and similarly unsure of what to expect. The teacher, a large woman wearing a sweatsuit and dangly earrings, was fidgeting around with her papers as we took our seats—the correct term would be "futzing," Sarah told me. As soon as twenty of us were assembled, she introduced herself.

"Welcome, everybody," she said with wide eyes. "My name's Ruth, and together we have quite a year ahead of us." She explained that she'd have us for the first ninety minutes of each three-hour class, after which a visiting rabbi would present a lecture. She then handed out a short survey—Where do you work? Who's your favourite Jew? What religion are you now?—which we were to fill out in block letters, hold up and use as a basis for mingling.

I filled in the line about occupation with perhaps too much detail—I could have said journalist and left it at that. Instead, I named my newspaper and position, recalling that my employer's strong pro-Israel stance had once come in handy when I was vying for an apartment. The Jewish landlord had even apologized for having a competing paper in his office, noting with embarrassment that he didn't know how it got there.

I realized later that this entered me into the teacher's bad books, as the paper is also a conservative one and she loudly self-identified as an anti-war, anti-American liberal. In a way, this was the first lesson I learned: if stereotypes are pretty useless in general, they're even more so when it comes to Jews, hence the old saw about two Jews having at least three opinions on any given subject.

As far as ice-breaking activities go, walking around the room with our lives scrawled out on questionnaires is a good one, though not one I'd recommend for cocktail parties, as the conversations tended to be along the lines of, "You're Catholic? Me too! But Woody's recent movies haven't been that great, huh?"

Still, a series of awkward conversations led us to sort the students as follows:

The jDate Couple. He was a skinny little Israeli guy; she was a Filipino Roman Catholic. Beauty and the Geek. When we were told to find people with similar religious backgrounds during our meet-and-greet, she and I quickly realized we had approximately nothing in common save for baptisms and an inherited allegiance to the Pope. They met online and ran a mysterious business out of the home. With no prompting, he explained that it was "very successful." They easily earned a spot on our Ones to Watch list.

The Odd Couple. She was a larger woman with a loud, gravelly voice. He was a skinny, quiet Trinidadian man. He was quite shy, but she made up for it. She doted on him and gently teased, which was funny and touching at the same time. Also on the Ones to Watch list.

The Power Couple. These were the lawyers—if not in actual occupation than at least in dress, demeanour and work ethic. He was Jewish, she wasn't. They had to make major sacrifices to get to the class for 7 p.m., but these were people who had no problem making major sacrifices. They'd set their minds to this, and that was that.

The Advanced Power Couple. Also lawyers, but with kids already. They didn't worry about conversion before the wedding because if the mother's Jewish, the children are too. Now he just wanted to understand what the kids were singing about.

The Couple You Can Relate to. She was a bubbly television producer. He was a former bush pilot studying to become a lawyer. They were engaged and ready to do it right. On some level, it was nice to think I could have been a bush pilot and still ended up in this class.

And then there was the teacher. I'd like to say we didn't immediately form an opinion of her, but the fact is she was wearing gemstone-encrusted purple Uggs. Being in a kids' classroom made us feel like we were regressing, but being at the head of it clearly had the opposite effect. She'd been doing this for decades and told us that past students were always calling her for Hebraic help; she also told us she would always be on call—anytime, day or night, her BlackBerry was by her side in case we forgot how to pronounce any letters of the Hebrew alphabet. We dutifully copied down the digits.

She then explained that she was a gastronomic Jew. That meant she loved to eat and insisted that each week two couples volunteer to bring food and drink to help us through the evening. She took names and handed us over to the first guest rabbi, a large-bellied, bearded holy man who looked just the way you'd hope a visiting rabbi would look. He opened things up with a question: "Who are the Jews? Are they a nation, a race, a culture or a religion?" He wrote those four categories on the board and waggled his eyebrows.

We didn't need the waggle to know this was a trick question. We paired off with a lawyer couple and went through the puzzle anyway. Ari and Susan approached the problem methodically. You could see how their sharp legal minds won cases and made their careers. I looked over at Sarah and caught her doodling in the margins of her notebook.*

"Let's start with nation," Ari said. "Obviously, the Jews were around before the state of Israel, so we can discount that definition of the word."

"But there is 'nation' in the sense of a people," Susan added.

"Like Quebec, or like Leafs Nation," I said, in reference to Toronto's lovably losing hockey team.

"Both Israel and the Leafs have a blue-and-white colour scheme," my Sarah said, briefly interrupting her sketch of the rabbi.

"But the Israelis win more often than the Leafs," I added.

"Point taken," Ari smiled. "Now, as for a race, you can't convert to a race. Plus, there are Jews from Europe, Africa, the Middle East, and so on."

I saw the opportunity to play up my scientific training, and though I remembered less and less with each passing year, I couldn't resist.

*See page ix, Sarah's Class Sketchbook

"But don't forget how useful the Ashkenazi Jews are to geneticists, what with all their diseases. Race doesn't really have a scientific definition beyond having a similar gene pool. Some Jews at least have that."

"Bio-boy over here," Sarah muttered, perhaps forgetting we were in front of other people. "And don't forget that if Ben's mother had been Jewish, we wouldn't be here."

"How about culture?" I said, quickly moving things along. "The Jews definitely have their klezmer music, kugels and special brand of Catskills comedy."

"True," Susan said. "But Spanish Jews wouldn't understand that and they don't even make kugel."

"Yes, if you think about food, that one doesn't quite work," Ari said. "Some Jews can eat rice on Passover, while others can't."

"So it has to be religion," I concluded. "I mean, that's what we're here to convert to, right?"

"But just because I haven't been to a synagogue in years, that doesn't make me less Jewish," Sarah said.

The rabbi told us our time was up and went around the room, taking everyone's answers and putting check marks under each category. Religion was the clear front-runner, but every category had a few votes.

"You're all right," the rabbi waggled, "but you're all missing something."

He then redrew his chalkboard diagram as a web, with religion at the centre and culture, nationalism and race around it.

"It's hard to define Judaism as any one of these, but altogether, we get pretty close."

He then explained that Jews were also known as people

of the covenant, meaning that they were defined under simple contract law. Was this a talking point designed for the class's many lawyers? They did seem to perk up for this argument.

It began with a *brit,* or covenant, between the big guy upstairs and the Jewish people. First, we clarify who's involved here: God is the Almighty, the Eternal one, the one and only deity who controls all of Heaven and Earth. The Jews are defined as a kingdom of priests, a holy people and a race that is to be a light to the nations. (Nations translates as "goyim," from which the word "goy" derives, from which many *Mad* magazine jokes derive. It was all coming together.)

Under the terms of this contract, God will

✡ give the Jews the land of Israel as an eternal possession. (At this point, I realized that this contract, even if set in actual stone, might not be enough for everyone.)

✡ provide sustenance and protection.

✡ make the Jews numerous. (Everything's relative, but fair enough.)

✡ cause the Jews to endure.

In return, the Jews will

✡ obey and do God's will, as outlined in the manual.

Seems like a pretty good deal—God has four clauses while the Jews have but one—until you have a look at the manual, also known as the Torah or the Jewish Bible, but not the Old Testament because, while it is both old and a testament, it's the only one we've got. In essence, this explanation defined Torah study as a reading of the fine print.

So, the rabbi said, the Jews are the people of the covenant, and that goes back to Abraham.

If anyone wants to become Jewish, they need only join the covenant. But how do you do that? Now we were getting to the meat of the matter: how would this year of classes actually make us Jewish? The question quickly turned into an Abbott-and-Costello routine.

"How do you become a Jew? By being born Jewish." He paused here to smile and waggle his eyebrows.

"But I wasn't. How can I become Jewish?"

"By being born Jewish." Smile, waggle.

"But I just told you I wasn't—now what?"

"By being born Jewish." That wasn't even grammatically correct, but he smiled and waggled after it anyway.

The point he eventually came to was that you had to be either born a Jew or born *again* a Jew, and the latter was the only option for all the previously born among us. The concept of being born again was briefly upsetting, for it brought to mind George W. Bush and teetotalling, but the rabbi explained that the concept began as a Jewish one.

"It's like the Jews invented everything," I whispered to Sarah.

"Maybe we did," she said. "Now shush, this is interesting."

The Jewish rebirth began with a year of study, though with the summer break it was actually more like nine months. Suddenly the kid-sized desks made sense. There (here) you learned about Jewish culture, traditions and Hebrew. Once that was completed, you went before the *beit din,* or house of judgment, where you had to prove that you understood the basics of Jewish law and rejected the tenets of your former faith (in other words, acknowledge that Jesus was no longer your homeboy). Three learned rabbis would quiz you on your intentions and preparations, and then adjourn to decide whether you were truly prepared.

Assuming you passed, it was then time for the rituals. After much idle speculation, this was the first formal explanation of the circumcision. Obviously, it's preferable to take care of that shortly after birth, when the whole world seems like such a post-womb letdown that one more cut doesn't hurt. But as the rabbi pointed out and our readings confirmed, the first Jew was in the same boat we were in. As a reading in our *Introduction to Judaism* textbook explained:

> *Abraham was forty-eight years old when he came to know his Creator. Yet he was not commanded to circumcise himself at that time and waited till he reached the age of ninety-nine (Genesis 17:24), in order not to shut the door in the face of proselytes, however advanced in years.*

Living to the age of ninety-nine before the invention of indoor plumbing seems bad enough, but having to perform your own circumcision before the invention of anaesthetic was enough to make even the rabbi wince.

And while it's nice that they welcome you to undergo painful surgery no matter how old you are, I was still relieved that my parents had made the right decision when I was born.

I looked casually around the classroom and wondered if anyone was unlucky enough to have to go through with the big cut. It should at least be worth some extra credit.

Why was this necessary in the first place? As the rabbi explained, it all came back to contract law. The Hebrew term for the procedure is *brit milah,* which translates as the covenant of circumcision. Part of the fine print of the original contract was that famous line about being fruitful and multiplying. Just in case the Jews forgot about that, or decided to get all fruitful without multiplying, this God-mandated scar was there to remind them of the contract.

In the event that the convert is already circumcised, they get to skip the genital-based rituals and go straight to the bagels and lox. At least, that's what I'd hoped to hear, but sadly there's a procedure called the *hatafat dam brit,* or drop of blood of the covenant. And this drop of blood is *not* drawn from the index finger. Before we could dwell on this thought, the rabbi changed the subject to the final ritual.

"How many of you have been baptized?" the rabbi asked. Half of us timidly raised our hands, worried that this would somehow relate to the circumcision discussion. "Well, the Christian baptism font is based on a Jewish concept, and that's the last thing a convert needs to do. You must completely immerse yourself in the waters, and then you become born again as a Jew."

You must be naked as the day you were born at this point, and there must be three Jews in the room, too. Still, the rabbi stressed it would be "private, and quite nice."

Once you towel off, you're a Jew. No one can take that away from you. There's no glass ceiling in Judaism, the rabbi explained, and Jews by birth are forbidden from singling out Jews by conversion. In fact, God loves you even more, and our text quotes a parable about a stag who decides to come live with a herd of sheep. When the shepherd tells the king about this, he's instructed to take special care of the stag, ensuring that it gets protection and water. When the shepherd asks why, the king explains:

> *The flock has no choice, for it is their nature to graze in the field all day and come in each night to sleep in the stable. Stags, however, sleep in the wilderness. It is not their nature to enter the living places of human beings. Shall we not consider it a merit for this one who has left behind all the vast wilderness, the place of all wild animals, and has come and stood in the yard?*

At this late point in the lecture, this stag was itching to get back out into the wilderness. My fellow antlered gentiles seemed similarly restless, and the rabbi took the hint and wrapped things up. As we filtered out of the classroom and made our way to the bus stop, I tried to put a positive spin on the class for Sarah.

"The lecture was good, don't you think?"

"Well, 'good' is a strong word. It took three hours to get about twenty minutes' worth of information across."

"Really?" I suddenly felt both stupid for sitting rapt for most of the lecture and defensive of the whole endeavour. "Not everyone's been to Hebrew school, you know."

"That's the point," Sarah said. "You haven't and I have, so why do we both need to be here? I'm behind on my cartoon this week, and I guess I will be every week from now on."

The bus pulled up and we got on and took our seats. We sat in silence until I couldn't bear it any longer, during which time the bus travelled less than two blocks.

"I'm doing this for you, though!" I whispered.

"Are you? I never asked you to, and we can get married without it. Our kids would still be Jewish. It's just, well, it's a lot of commitment for a nice idea that maybe should just be an idea."

"No. I'm not going to quit now, not after I've told everyone."

"Are you doing it for me or for everyone?"

"That's not fair. It is for you, it's just . . . when I commit to doing something, I want to do it completely and do it right."

"I know that, and I love that about you, but I just think you can't let your determination to get this done stop you from thinking about why you're doing it."

"Okay, okay. I don't want to fight, especially not on the bus. And we're here, anyway."

We stepped off the bus and entered the subway station, making our way down to the platform.

"I'm sorry," I said. "Everything you've said is right, and I will think about it some more. But can you bear with me?"

"Of course I can. I'll see through anything you want to see through, but you need to see things from my perspective, too."

"Deal."

The subway pulled into our station.

"I can help you finish your cartoon," I said as we walked up to the street. "It'll be like in *Family Circus,* when the dad is on vacation and little Billy scrawls his version of events."

"I'd be happy if you just copyedited it for me."

Who's in Charge Here?

I don't think I have problems with authority, but then I'm sure most prison inmates would say the same thing—that it's authority that has a problem with them. I've never done time and I don't plan to, largely because I get along fine within society's rules as long as I'm treated like an adult. At a certain precocious point—mid-adolescence, I think—I started to really bristle at any power dynamic I didn't completely understand.

This made the job of being my father a tricky one, and the man already has a tricky job. He is a heart surgeon, which means that he earns his living saving lives. Using suture, forceps and a horrific clamping device that keeps the rib cage open, he regularly leads a team of highly trained professionals into the patient's chest, bypassing clogged arteries and replacing faulty valves.

It's an incomprehensible thing to do for a living, especially to his children. I could never really square the dad I knew with the man who held human hearts in his hands on a daily basis. Adolescents are supposed to go from seeing their parents as infallible to seeing them as completely flawed. While the screaming matches that led to my parents' divorce certainly displayed their faults to us kids, I never really figured my father out. This was a man who once burned his mouth with Comet industrial cleanser when we'd run out of toothpaste, so I knew he wasn't perfect. Yet the occasions when I'd meet his eternally grateful patients were reminders that many people saw him as a saint. Add to that his humble beginnings—after leaving the air force, my grandfather worked as a school janitor; my father put himself through school bagging groceries—and he's practically on the fast track toward beatification.

He could do plenty of wrong in my eyes, of course. For instance, when our bicycles were stolen from the garage in high school, my brother and I had planned to go buy new ones together with the insurance money. The next day, Dad came home with new bikes for both of us. We were thankful, obviously, but I grumbled afterward about being cut out of the selection process. (I realize, of course, that there isn't a violin small enough to play for this perceived slight.) Similarly, he'll often give art and clothes as gifts, the sorts of things that are almost entirely dependent on personal taste, or perform hugely generous acts like sending his mother on an all-expenses paid trip to visit her sister in England, then having her dilapidated kitchen completely remodelled while she was abroad. The gesture is a kind one, but I can't help but think the action is a carry-over from the operating room: this is the right thing to do, I'm responsible for getting it done and time is of the essence. Does it matter if extensive consultations are omitted from the process? That dedication to expediency is what you want in your surgeon, but in a father it can be a bit stifling.

In a roundabout sort of way, this explains my path toward medical school. My father loves his work and excels at it, and I had the marks to follow him. Of course, I preferred newsprint over organic chemistry, and that put me in a bind that came to a crux in a long conversation with my college roommate, Ryan, after I finished my magazine internship—the highlight of which was my construction of a crossword puzzle. (Admittedly, it broke some of the rules of the form—two-letter clues are sniffed at by most cruciverbalists—but still, it was a thrill to see my byline next to such a complex pattern of squares and words.)

"I can't believe I could do something like that for a living," I told Ryan.

"And why wouldn't you?"

"It just seems like—well, shouldn't I be trying to do something bigger than a crossword puzzle?"

"Like what? Saving lives like your father?"

"Well, yeah. Isn't that more meaningful?"

"What is more meaningful, really?" Ryan asked. As usual, our conversation was segueing into an undergraduate philosophy seminar. "If someone's heart is repaired, they can return to their regular life. But what do they do to enjoy that life? Crossword puzzles give millions of people enjoyment and meaning."

"Are you saying a crossword puzzle is equivalent to a coronary bypass?"

"Not an equivalence, of course, but one isn't necessarily morally superior to the other."

For me, the stumbling block had been that I hadn't stopped to consider that anything I would enjoy doing might be in any way comparable to saving lives. I realized then that my limited frame of reference was discounting approximately 98 percent of human endeavour. Climbing a mountain because it's there is nice and all, but whose life does it save? Enriching lives was equally important, I began to think. Such insights culminated in my eventual decision not to go to medical school.

My mother saw the decision as a repudiation of my father, and I began to worry that this would be one of those rare situations when he'd agree with her interpretation. During those two months between my move back from Montreal and my accepting the newspaper job, I was still living under his roof. I broke the news gingerly, around the same time I announced that, with my raise and year-long contract, I'd be moving into my own place. He was supportive, to be sure, but I wasn't convinced he understood my decision. He hinted that perhaps my friends had talked me into not going, but these were only hints.

Despite living in the same city, we grew apart. From time to time he would stop by my apartment with lavish gifts, which I began to actively disdain. The occasional family dinners were awkward affairs, not least because he was in the process of separating from his long-time girlfriend. Having medical school in common would have brought us together, I always thought, and now not having it seemed to give licence to an equal and opposite effect. I wanted some resolution, but didn't know how to get it. In the first three years of my new life, our interactions became rarer and rarer (and more strained when they did take place). Eventually, I decided no relationship at all was better than what we had.

Without my father in my life, my only real authority figures were at the office.

I realized early on that a bit of audacity went a long way in dealing with my superiors, assuming my work backed it up. I occasionally overdid it, leading to a performance review that listed my main shortcoming as contemptuousness, but the net effect was a series of promotions and the sometimes-grudging respect of my bosses. I gradually came to realize that, as an adult making a decent living, I answered to no one outside of the office. I can't say I didn't enjoy that. When I accepted an editor's job, it dawned on me that I was now unambiguously in charge. Becoming an authority figure furthered my resolve to keep my father out of my life. This was roughly equivalent to my decision to stop looking at my marks during my fourth year at university. Paying attention to them was so stressful that I decided, enough! I would go to class and study as best I could, but I wouldn't get caught up in worrying over the letter grades. This was a ludicrous strategy, but at the time it seemed like a great relief. The same was true of my paternal estrangement.

I went on in this state for about a year. By that point, I began to realize how untenable it was. Eventually, there would be a family wedding or a funeral that I would have to attend, and an uncomfortable situation would be made more so. It also made things very tense for my brother and sister: not only did they have parents who became visibly upset when the other was mentioned, but their elder brother was similarly aligned. Finally, what kind of a person was I to do this? I recognized my mother's anxiety and tried to help her as best I could, but my father wasn't permitted his own faults because they rubbed me the wrong way? In a sudden burst of conscience, I phoned him and asked if he'd go to a family therapist with me. He agreed, of course, and in the kindly lady's home office, I went through my litany of real and imagined concerns and complaints, from the bike I wasn't able to pick out to the elephant in the room that was medical school. Fundamentally, I explained, I just wanted us to be equals, and I wanted that to happen without my having to perform open-heart surgery by his side. I realized that many of my grievances sounded silly, but I hoped the cumulative weight would at least suggest why our relationship had become so difficult. My father seemed surprised by some of my comments, and slightly wounded by others, but I had to admit his case was a strong one. He had raised us as best he could, and if he were able to do it over again, he would do it better. There was no definitive resolution, and the only closure that we arrived at was my abandonment of the silent treatment.

Three years later, when I phoned to tell him about the engagement and my plans to convert, he was completely supportive. He would certainly be there and would help us out in any way we needed him to, and really, what more could I want? It seemed like the wrong time to insist upon splitting the wedding bill.

I wasn't particularly proud of the kind of son I'd been, but I was relatively satisfied with where we had ended up. My father now knew what bugged me, and I had some understanding of why he did what he did. He was still my father, but now we were both adults.

There was no such equal footing to be found in Ruth's classroom. When I took my kiddie seat beside my wife-to-be, I realized this would be my first time as a student since university. Sarah was right about the lessons being repetitive and slow, but there was more to it. Once I began to see how Ruth ran the class, I realized it would also be my first adult experience of accepting someone's authority outside of work.

Ruth at first seemed like a relaxed, informal speaker who had no problem wandering off the syllabus to tell us about her life. With her garish sweatsuits and her insistence on snack breaks, she furthered the impression that we were back in kindergarten. It seemed kind of fun—maybe not the scholarly introduction to Judaism I had envisioned, but that was apparently the domain of the guest speaker.

Early on, Susan, one of the corporate lawyers and her couple's Jew-in-training, arrived late for class. She was six minutes tardy and made her entrance on exaggerated tiptoes, her face in a penitent grimace—both acts meant to signal her apology. Ruth interrupted her musings on the many kinds of Jewish food she enjoyed to chastise the latecomer.

"You know, one of the rules of this class is arriving on time. I could lock the door right at seven if I wanted to."

"Ruth, I'm sorry, I rushed to get here but I was stuck in a meeting with a senior partner and just couldn't get out."

"This class has to be a priority in your life. It's not fair to me or your classmates when you're late."

"I realize that, but—"

"We can talk about this later. After class."

Susan took her seat next to Ari, an intense guy under normal circumstances. He was glowering at Ruth. She didn't seem to pay any heed. I looked away before he saw that I'd noticed.

Later in that lesson, Ruth turned on the charm, as if to convince students surprised by her outburst that she was still the friendly lady she'd been back at the beginning.

"Remember," she said at the end of the lecture, "you have my number and my email, so call me whenever you need. I've been doing this for twenty-four years, and I still get calls from students who need help with their Hebrew. I'm just a phone call away."

There was no rabbi's lecture that night, which was just as well. We'd easily packed three hours of drama into ninety minutes. The offending couple offered us a ride home, a voyage that could have been powered entirely by the force of their combined anger.

"I would understand if I'd come half an hour late into an important lecture about the Torah, but honestly, she was talking about her favourite foods!" Susan vented.

"It was completely ridiculous," I concurred from the back seat. "Just like being back in kindergarten."

"Even Hebrew school wasn't that bad," Sarah said.

From the front passenger seat, Ari spoke in a low voice. "We said we were going to do this thing, and we're going to do it. That doesn't mean we have to take any crap from her."

On one level, I agreed with him, though I realized I might just take a bit of crap if it meant avoiding conflict. I didn't care for Ruth's teaching style, her behaviour or her sequined sweaters, but I made the decision to put these differences aside, keep my head down and power through the class. I resolved to never be late and gave Sarah a secret message in the form of a hand squeeze.

"So, what shul did you guys say you were at?" Sarah asked, correctly interpreting my signal to change the subject.

Of course, if the beginning of these classes introduced a new authority figure into our lives, it wasn't really Ruth. Nor was it our scholarly rabbi, with whom we would exchange awkward hellos and *shabbat shaloms* after the two services a month we made a point of attending. No, the real boss we had to answer to now, as a newly reobservant Jew and a Jew-in-training, was the big man upstairs. This was where Reform Judaism became a bit tricky. What the rabbi said in the beginning was correct: you don't have to believe. But if you admit this up front, how do you pray?

"What do you think about when you're praying?" I asked Sarah as we were leaving the synagogue one Friday evening.

"I try to read the Hebrew parts, I guess, and translate them into English."

"But aren't they sort of ridiculous? God is wonderful and God is great and we don't deserve to be in God's presence, repeated over and over again?"

"I know, it can be hard to take if you focus on it like that. You have to relax into it and sort of meditate, I suppose. Once you hear them a few thousand times, you're more used to the rhythms than the words."

"So you just turn off your brain? That seems kind of silly. And how immature is God that he needs us to constantly tell us how powerful he is?"

"Why don't you ask the rabbi these questions?" Sarah

replied, mildly annoyed at having been made defender of the faith.

It turned out that I didn't need to; a visiting rabbi at class the next week took up my arguments—without prompting—in a lecture on prayer. "Why does God need our affirmation?" he asked. "He doesn't! We're doing all this chanting for ourselves. Otherwise, we tend to forget how to be humble." By way of explanation, this learned Jew held up his Motorola RAZR phone. "Isn't this amazing?" he asked. Indeed, although it wasn't WiFi-enabled, it was a pretty slick telecommunications device. Then, lest we mistake him for a sales associate at Best Buy, came the follow-up question: "What do you think 'false idols' refers to?"

Humans, he went on to explain, have an enormous capacity for hubris. We love to worship the work of our own hands, something we can control; ultimately, we're worshipping ourselves. This is where the genius of Jewish prayer is apparent, so sayeth the rabbi. However temporarily, it takes the focus off ourselves. It isn't about authority *among* humans; it's about authority *over* humans. It sounds quite nice in the half-sung Hebrew, but when you read the translation, the message hits you like stone tablets dropped from the sky. He had us read the concluding part of the Amidah, the central prayer of Judaism:

> *We acknowledge to You, O Lord, that You are our God,*
> *as You were the God of our ancestors, forever and ever.*
> *Rock of our life, Shield of our help, You are immutable*
> *from age to age. We thank You and utter Your praise,*
> *for our lives that are delivered into Your hands, and*
> *for our souls that are entrusted to You; and for Your*

miracles that are with us every day and for your mar-velously kind deeds that are of every time; evening and morning and noon-tide. Thou art good, for Thy mer-cies are endless: Thou art merciful, for Thy kindnesses never are complete: from everlasting we have hoped in You. And for all these things may Thy name be blessed and exalted always and forevermore. And all the living will give thanks unto Thee and praise Thy great name in truth, God, our salvation and help. Selah. Blessed be Thou, O Lord, Thy name is good, and to Thee it is meet to give thanks.

It's not easy to say that if you're not sure that there is a God, I had told Sarah. But that, the rabbi explained, was to miss the point. God doesn't need our validations; the prayer is about us. Most importantly, the prayer acknowledges something bigger than us. Does it need to be so repetitive? Apparently, yes. Humility requires it. In a nice interfaith aside, he noted at this point that the word "Islam" means "submission" for the same reasons.

In class, I wasn't as bold as I had been with our rabbi, but I had the same question. What if I don't believe in God or His authority? What if I wanted to follow what the old bumper-sticker slogans said and Question Authority? I didn't ask this question, but one of the more aggressive lawyers did.

This rabbi's answer was the same as the one I originally heard: Judaism is about what you do, not what you believe. What matters is not that you believe in the prayer, but that you pray in the first place. Don't focus on what the structures are meant to do; focus on the structures themselves. If you do it, you believe it.

The emphasis on actions over belief is a natural extension of the contract-law explanation our rabbi gave us in our first class, and it explains why, for Jews, the words "religion" and "faith" aren't synonymous. In a way, the soft sell seems more grown-up: instead of insisting on belief first, you insist on action. This, I began to realize, was the kind of authority I didn't mind. It wasn't asking too much: I can say the prayers and I can even find something soothing in their repetition. And when you stop worrying about whether you believe in God or not, He's much easier to get along with.

Passover Worth Passing Over

In my years as Sarah's non-Jewish boyfriend, my main exposure to her religion came on Passover. On that holiday in early spring, the Lazarovics would make a pilgrimage to Debbie's sister's house in the suburbs of Ottawa. That's where Sandy lived with Michael, her second husband, and it's where the festivities were held. Partly this was because Sandy was the only relative with the centrally located space to host the clan, and partly because she taught hospitality at the local college and thus knew a thing or two about hosting. Like her sister, she was kind, generous and prone to breaking into dance when the inspiration struck. Michael was a former taxi dispatcher who used his natural gift with numbers to become a world-recognized expert on Oracle software. He considered a black T-shirt to be formal attire, and at their wedding, the *chuppah*—the canopy under which a Jewish bride and groom are formally wed—was sewn to look like the cover of Pink Floyd's *Dark Side of the Moon* album. Early in my relationship with Sarah, Michael crashed at my apartment in Toronto while in town for a conference and stayed up late drinking tonic water and telling my roommate, Jason, and I that if we wanted to get high sniffing glue (we didn't), there was a certain colour of label to look for. We found this quite amusing at the time. Sandy and Michael celebrated their love with inside-joke vanity plates, his reading YATFG—"you are the fucking guy"—and hers reading YAFTG. I still don't quite get it, but as none of the Lazarovics do, I figure I'm in good company.

After three years of Passover attendance, I had the sequence of events down pat. We took the train in on the day of, and upon arriving sat on the couch drinking screwdrivers with Marsha. Sandy's kids and Michael's kids arrived, as well as Michael's nerdy brother and his charming mother, who was of the generation that "took a newspaper" rather than subscribed to one. This came up every year as she explained that she didn't take my paper.

Cocktails were served shortly after, and if Jake was lucky enough to get a quorum of his daughters, he would needle them about career plans and life prospects. As an interested third party, I always found this amusing and would help things along.

"Jake, did you know that Sarah recently received a grant to make a short film?" I would posit as I popped a jujube in my mouth (our hostess's profession ensured that there were dishes of candy and nuts in the living room.)

"Sarah, why didn't you tell us this?" Jake would ask as Sarah rolled her eyes.

"It's not a big deal! I don't even know what it's going to be yet!"

In this manner, I both teased Sarah and established myself as an important conduit of information about his daughter's activities. The Seder, as the dinner is called, followed a script observed by Jewish families around the world. Sandy and Debbie both made brisket and pretended to argue over whose was better.* I would play along and pronounce it a dead heat. Michael's brother tried to ensure that all the prayers were said in the right order and to the fullest extent; Michael did his best to curtail his brother's thoroughness and keep the wait between courses as short as possible. The kids' table drank plenty of wine, and before we knew it the Seder was done. Sandy's best students were hired to help with the cleanup and everything was packed away by 10 p.m.

This is my secular version of Passover, one that doesn't really touch upon the meaning of the event. The holiday itself marks the liberation of the Jews from Egypt and their subsequent wandering through the desert; because there wasn't time to let the bread rise, matzoh is eaten; because the slaves cried bitter tears, there are bitter herbs; because the slaves built temples for their masters, there's a delicious paste of nuts and honey. It's one big meal as metaphor, and if some of the comparisons aren't obvious, they are at least tasty.

Now that I was officially learning how to be a Jew, a bit more rigour was expected of my Passover. For starters, I was to call it by its Hebrew name, Pesach. Ruth spent several weeks describing the importance of the holiday—the removal of all leavened bread from the house, the importance of having enough prayer books at the table, the significance of having an orange at the table to

*See pages 263–265

represent women. We recited the relevant prayers over and over again in hopes of impressing the Jews around our Seder tables. The preparations culminated in a very special "Pesach workshop" held a week before the holiday at a synagogue we'd never been to. I was looking forward to it the same way that I used to look forward to field trips at school: it's still school, but at least there's a change of venue.

The seminar took place on secluded grounds in a well-to-do suburban neighbourhood. This was to be the lesson that explained exactly why this night was unlike all the others. I took a taxi from work and waited for Sarah to carpool up with some classmates. There were several classes attending the evening, which led the organizers to divide us up into groups named after letters of the Hebrew alphabet. This was the first sign that the intellectual rigour of the evening would be in short supply, as would the screwdrivers. I chose the letter *gimmel* and phoned Sarah several times to make sure I wasn't attending alone.

She eventually arrived, and we filed into the auditorium. There would be four activity stations for our four groups to visit. At one station, we would learn to roll matzoh balls for use in soup; another involved dipping matzoh in chocolate, with the option of caramel left to our discretion; a third matzoh-based activity involved gluing four sheets of unleavened bread together to make a vase; and finally, for any leftover matzoh, we could make a cloth envelope decorated with a variety of ribbons. Afterward, there would be a short lecture, but the focus was most definitely on technique ahead of Torah.

All these stations were manned by well-meaning but humourless volunteers, and the interactions ranged from me being lightly chastised for an overly generous application of glitter to a stern rebuke of Susan, who dared whisper to her husband while the matzoh-ball-rolling demo was taking place.

"If everyone could please be quiet and respectful," the volunteer said with a disapproving look in the direction of the whisperers, "we can all get a chance to see how matzoh balls are made."

At that point, we decided to go with the flow. There were plenty of books that would explain the meaning of Pesach, why we lean to the left during the meal (because we are no longer slaves and are allowed to recline, I later learned), what the four questions mean, etc., but how many august volumes of Judaica could provide precise instruction about writing the word "matzoh" in glitter? In between stations, there was a cantor leading groups in Passover songs. She was easily the most charismatic person in the temple. Sarah and I agreed that this was an evening better suited to third-graders, but that it was basically harmless fun.

But just when we'd prepared to shift our brains into idle, the arts-and-crafts portion of the evening wrapped up. We were all summoned back into the main auditorium, and the rabbi, our host, was introduced with profound adoration by the head volunteer, who described her as the best thing that ever happened to their synagogue. For me, the most appealing part of Reform Judaism is its love of logic: because the rabbis have spent thousands of years questioning everything we do, there is always a line of reasoning behind every ritual. The rabbi that evening threw out those notes to speak from the heart. And what a weird heart it was.

For her, Passover was a passionate time, one that seemed to send sensual shivers of holiness down her spine. She told us about her most memorable Passover, on which she and her husband had just moved to a new apartment and, without any furniture, sat opposite each other on the floor, stared into each other's souls and read Torah aloud all night long. "Pesach" means "mouth open," she said, and we can be redeemed with words, the conversation lifting into holiness over hours and hours in a bare apartment. She described this tantric worship in slow, breathy tones, with her eyes closed.

At this point, I looked around the room to see how this erotic celebration of the time of liberation was sitting with everyone else. Lo and behold, all the matrons who had been manning the glue guns were rapt in attention. It was clear that this rabbi's visceral connection to her faith was by no means limited to Passover, and that it was much appreciated by her congregation.

As we left the shul, Sarah told me an old Jewish joke that I finally completely understood. It goes like this: A Jew is stranded on a desert island, as characters in jokes always are. When he's finally found, his rescuers notice two rudimentary structures built of palm leaves and bark. They ask why he's built two huts—surely one would have been sufficient to protect him from the elements—and he explains: "This one's my shul, and this one's the shul I wouldn't be caught dead in."

That night, we'd found the shul we wouldn't be caught dead in. Our experience there wasn't terrible, but it didn't exactly enhance my understanding of Passover. I looked forward to our trip to the Lazarovic Pesach, the train tickets to which I'd wisely booked a month in advance. I even had a matzoh vase and glitter-glued matzoh envelope to present to Sandy.

The day before we left, I asked Sarah when the rest of her family would be arriving.

"What do you mean? I told you they're not."

"Pardon?"

"I told you this when you booked the tickets a month ago. My parents have been back and forth so much dealing with my grandmother's estate that they decided to stay in Florida. Becky's in China and Jane's not coming up from Ithaca."

"So . . . it's just us?"

"Us and Sandy and Michael and his kids and my cousins, yes."

So we took the train up to Ottawa as per tradition, and as per tradition, Michael picked us up at the station.

"Hello, Berrett," he said with a bear hug. "Glad you guys could make it."

"Thanks for hosting us again," I said as I hoisted Sarah's bags into the trunk of the YATFG-plated car.

"Too bad you'll be the only Lazarovics here. Or would it be Lazarovi in the plural?"

"Either is fine," Sarah said.

"One Lazarovic, two Lazarovi," Michael riffed. "What would you call a collective of Lazarovi?"

"A frazzle?" I offered.

"A frazzle, yessir. You know where we have to go? Golden Palace. You can't come to Ottawa without Golden Palace egg rolls. World famous, but not kosher. Not even a bit."

"We're leaving tomorrow, though," Sarah protested.

"Then we'll go on the way to the train station. You'll get a bag, the Sweet Thing and I will get a bag, and everyone will be happy. Except maybe everyone on the train who smells them but doesn't get to have one."

He rambled on like this for the rest of the drive, a stream-of-consciousness babble that was just shy of being composed entirely of non sequiturs. Sandy welcomed us as warmly as ever and we went straight into cocktail hour. I ended up next to Michael's brother on the sofa. He didn't free-associate quite as proficiently as Michael and spent most of the evening extolling the virtues of several horrid sitcoms. When the Seder began, we were once again at the kids' table, but without Sarah's siblings. That meant we were immersed in a discussion of ultimate fighting, a subject of passionate interest to Michael's daughter's boyfriend. We followed along as best we could.

The next morning, we realized we were the only house guests. Michael and Sandy were going about their routines, and the holiday remnants were almost all gone. The night before, I had spoken fondly of the *matzoh brei,* the traditional breakfast scramble of the flourless bread and eggs, and Sandy whipped plates up for Michael and us. At that point I felt quite ridiculous, having come all this way to force Sarah's aunt to prepare me a Jewish breakfast. We ate quickly, thanked our hosts and helped load up the dishwasher. Sarah and I excused ourselves to pack up our stuff.

"So, was that weird?" I asked as we stripped the sheets.

"What, the *matzoh brei*?" Sarah asked. "I think it's weird to eat it with cinnamon, but Michael has the right idea with his hot sauce."

"No, you frazzle, you know what I mean. Is it weird that we're the only ones here from your family? You have to admit, it would be weird if, say, we crashed Thanksgiving at my uncle's house."

"No! First of all, my aunt would gladly have us visit no matter the holiday. And it's Jewish tradition to have strangers come to your Seder table. Not that we're strangers, but you know. And you really wanted to come for your Jewish education."

"Well, 'really' is a strong word. I mean, I didn't *not* want to come, but . . . well, I guess part of my Jewish education is trying to figure out your family, and it doesn't really work if they're not here."

"Well, you can figure out Michael, and then explain him to the rest of us."

We dragged our stuff out to the car, kissed Sandy goodbye and headed to Golden Palace en route to the train. The egg rolls were perhaps the greasiest I'd ever eaten, with pork and what might have been ground beef interspersed with the fillings.

"Man, they should sell that as an air freshener," Michael said as the car filled with the egg-roll aroma. We said our farewells and boarded the train.

Errett's Israel

At this point, life as a Jew in training accounted for a mere four hours of my week. There were three hours of class to attend each Tuesday night, and synagogue for an hour or so every other week. The remainder consisted of Hebrew homework, which in the early days comprised nothing more than memorizing the four letters we had learned and training myself to read from right to left. I realized my natural inclination to open a book the "normal" way betrayed me as a gentile in temple, and I had resolved to correct it.

Our nicely compartmentalized Jewish experience likely wasn't what the class organizers had in mind—the title of the textbook *Living a Jewish Life* certainly didn't suggest you could do so in just a few minutes each day—but it was ideal for Sarah and me. We didn't need to have big philosophical debates about what we'd learned or how we'd worship; we implicitly agreed that Ruth was over the top, that we liked our rabbi and that Judaism would bring us closer together.

That said, I was still waiting for that bolt from the blue. When was I going to get that rush of certainty that makes converts to anything, be it religion, jogging or vegetarianism, so annoying? I was grateful that the conversion process was so agreeable, but did that mean I was doing something wrong? In Sarah's view, it was just fine. In the beginning, she had confessed, she worried that her faith had not been strong enough to warrant my team-switching. That was why she had been vaguely embarrassed. Now that she'd seen things to be orderly and undemanding, she was relieved. She began looking at the whole endeavour as a way to learn about religion from a grown-up perspective, a chance to question and discuss the lectures and sermons she had taken as the Jewish equivalent of gospel truth in Hebrew school. And even reading all the little stories on the wall in the third-grade classroom was pleasantly diverting.

"Pleasantly diverting?" I asked her. "I agree, but weren't you hoping for something more?"

"You mean from the children's assignments? I think they're pretty sophisticated for third graders."

"You know what I mean. This whole class, the induction into a major religion. I'm glad it's manageable, too, but . . . well, maybe I'm not entirely glad. I guess what I'm wondering is, where's the awe?"

"Since when are you looking for awe? You could say Ruth is full of awe, as in awe-full. I don't really need awe. I need to get out of class on time and finish all my assignments by Wednesday so I can work on my movies for the rest of the week. This is educational, and a meaningful thing for us to do together, but I'm quite happy to keep it simple."

"Yeah, maybe you're right," I replied, agreeing with everything my fiancée had said but not entirely comfortable with it.

The lessons were definitely useful. When our Jewish friends would ask about what I'd learned, I would gladly show off my knowledge of Judaica, often stumping them in the process.

"Rachel, do you have any big plans for *Tu b'Shevat?*"

"Is it *Tu b'Shevat* already? Wait, which one's that?"

"The birthday of the trees, duh! It's the annual occasion on which the tax collector would visit your property to assess its agricultural yield."

"Wait a minute, that's not an important holiday!"

"As the first holiday we learned about, it's actually very important to me. To everyone else, not so much. We don't actually have *Tu b'Shevat* plans."

Of course, the limits of my knowledge were many, and it only took a Hebrew phrase or two to throw me off my game. Queries from less observant Jews and nonreligious friends always seemed to be slightly more suspicious.

"How's your class going?" my cubicle-mate, Maryam, would ask.

"So far, so good." There would be a pause, during which I realized she wasn't sure what else to say and I worried that she thought I was becoming hyperdevout and bringing my religion into the workplace. Obviously, I was projecting, but I only began to realize that after the fact.

"It's mostly history and vocab, really," I added. "And the big lesson so far is that Judaism is about what you do, not what you believe, so it's really just like going back to school."

"Okay," she responded, perhaps wondering why I was justifying the class to her. "What do you do?"

"Sorry?"

"You say it's about what you do and not what you believe, so what are you actually doing?"

"Ah, good question. Well, to tell the truth, not too much yet."

Conversations like that began to spread word around the office. This had an immediate positive effect in the form of an all-expenses-paid trip to Israel, offered to me by the weekend editor. The point was to write a travel feature on whichever parts of the country we chose, but it was offered to me for more specific reasons.

"I heard about your conversion, which I think is great," she'd said. "It's wonderful to see you doing that for Sarah. If you're up for this trip, maybe it can help you along."

I wasn't quite doing it for Sarah, of course, but why quibble over a gift horse? A trip to the home of the Jews: this was where the awe must be. I had always thought religious pilgrims were a bit nutty, but maybe there was something to it. I didn't want a reawakening, just a bit of religious motivation. Surely Israel could provide that.

Admittedly, in my limited experience, press trips—junkets, to use the J-word—tended to be agonizing affairs. They have the look and feel of a vacation but the itinerary of a dull industry conference. The ethics of junkets are generally fishy as well: you're enjoying the hospitality of your hosts, so it hardly seems polite to return home and publish an article pointing out that the pool ought to have been a few degrees warmer. Not that I would want to crack the front page with such an exposé, but the effect of knowing you can't say something just makes you want to blurt it out.

But this was different. This was the Holy Land. Sarah's father, Jake, was born in Haifa and still had family there. He had a list of relatives for us to visit and urged us to make plans with them before the trip was even confirmed.

Sarah's burgeoning career as a professional illustrator made it feasible to invite her along as my artist, and we began to plan our trip. This would be a tour of cosmopolitan Israel, we decided. We had taken a Roman holiday the year before and found that, after three days in the Eternal City, we were jonesing for the not-so-eternal part. We would pre-empt that mistake in Israel by declaring our focus to be on new art, design, literature and—cleverest of all—food, the very opposite of dusty tombs and crowded historical sites.

These things were indeed included in the itinerary prepared for us by the ministry of tourism, but then there was little that wasn't on the list. During one week in April, we were to be taken all over the historic homeland of the Jews: from Tel Aviv to Caesarea to Haifa to Tzfat to the Sea of Galilee to Masada to the Dead Sea to Jerusalem.* We were happy to see we would be on a private tour; if hell is in fact other people, there's a special circle comprised of slovenly freeloading junketeers. Our own private guide would whisk us around the world's most contentious nation.

Unsurprisingly, Gaza and the West Bank weren't on the agenda, but then this was a tourism trip and not a fact-finding mission. And, to be honest, I wasn't that interested in delving into the never-ending debates about Israel. This was a stance I

*See page 266

had quickly adopted at my university paper. Though the volumes of tit-for-tat correspondence from Hillel and the Palestinian Students Association easily filled our letters page, the arguments tended to focus on historical boundaries and land claims beyond the mandate of any extracurricular organization. I was willing to concede that an impartial observer who had spent many years in the region talking to people on all sides— as opposed to both sides, a generalization that overlooks the many shades of opinion in between the extremes—would have valid and interesting points to make. As it was, I wasn't ready to venture much beyond an opinion that both the Israelis and the Palestinians deserved their own strife-free homelands. Was that really so difficult? If I was to be a Jew, I realized I would need some more nuanced views.

It would be Sarah's fifth trip to Israel, so she wasn't anticipating a horizon-broadening experience. She'd visit her cousins, practise her Hebrew and enjoy a week in a sunny climate with her betrothed. We flew out of New York on El Al, and after aggressive security questioning (Why would you want to go during the national Independence Day? Uh, why wouldn't we?), were allowed to sit in the King David Lounge. When we touched down at Ben Gurion many hours later, there was no joyous singing of the national anthem, as I'd heard there might be.

We were whisked through security and soon after collected by Nurit, our guide, and Ehad, our burly driver. We piled into their minivan and were off to Tel Aviv. After about twenty minutes of small talk, we independently realized that Nurit was, in a way, Ruth's Israeli counterpart. A tough-looking middle-aged woman with a slightly incongruous pixie haircut, she was very nice, but knowledgeable only in the most annoying and didactic way. Thankfully, it didn't take long to get to the hotel. From our room we had a view of the Mediterranean, with the sounds of paddleball players and smells of the beach wafting in as we took a jet-lagged mid-afternoon nap, happy to have made it halfway around the world.

In retrospect, I claim to have been quite happy at that moment in time, something Sarah disputes. In her memory I was grumpy for the entire trip. Not the case, I have insisted, but she was there and she would know. The first afternoon and evening were perfectly pleasant, though they gave us a hint of things to come. We strolled along the New Port boardwalk with Nurit and Ehad until we arrived at a seafood restaurant. The view over the Mediterranean was lovely, as was the food, particularly the prune-stuffed sea bass that Sarah had ordered and I had eaten off her plate. The dinner conversation, however, made me feel like the lonely paddleball player practising against a wall. Every line of inquiry was met with a cliché. Ehad spoke only a few words of English, so our attention went to Nurit. She too was a convert, someone who would understand what I was going through and could provide insight.

"I'm really hoping to understand Judaism better on this trip," I explained.

"Israel is the only place you can understand that. That's why I made *aliyah*," she replied, using the Hebrew term for a return to the promised land.

"Right. Well, I'm not there yet, but who knows what will happen on this trip."

"Israel is like no other country on earth. You'll see."

"This restaurant actually reminds me a bit of Italy," I said. "It's not like Italy."

"I think he just means the view and the food," Sarah said.

"This chef is Israeli," she said. The tone wasn't standoffish, per se; it seemed more like she was trying to be helpful but didn't quite know how. Then again, our wits may have been dulled by the fourteen-hour flight. We changed the subject to the food, which we all agreed was delicious.

Citing jet lag, we went back to our hotel room early to rest before heading out on our own to the main drag to see the Independence Day celebrations. We walked down to the festivities, passing fragrant gardens and overhearing bits of patio conversation in English, French and Hebrew. The streets and cafés were filled with young people and the skies were lit up. I noticed the Bauhaus buildings, white against the night sky, and the smells of street food. I made sure we visited a supermarket, always among my first stops in a strange place, to get a sense of the candy selection. My particular preference has always been gummi candy, the Sour Patch Kids, Orchard Pears, Fuzzy Peaches, Cherry Blasters and other fine Canadian-made confections. (For the sake of clarity, my mother refers to this whole suite of products simply as Woolly Mammoths, a term that is at once nonsensical and completely appropriate.) In North America, the quality of starch-based gummies far outweighs that of the gelatin-based variety, your gummi bears and gummi worms, etc. In Europe, I've found the inverse to be true: their sour belts aren't remotely competitive with ours, but the gummi bears made by Haribo in Germany are the originals and the best. In Israel, I found the best of all worlds, plus some brands I'd never seen before. I happily parted with my shekels and we continued our stroll until the sugar wore off and we were ready to crash.

"I had a great time in Tel Aviv!" I later insisted to Sarah.

"Yeah, for the first half-day, and mostly due to gummies. Then you started complaining," she would say, not incorrectly.

The first irritant was the unnecessarily early wakeup call. Did we really need to be in the minivan by 8 a.m.? That hardly left time for breakfast, which was a novelty at each hotel. There was some mixture of a bacon-less Full English, the standard continental and the traditional Israeli breakfast of chopped salad, various cheeses, toast and eggs. I enjoyed taking my plate around the buffet to create the perfect cross-cultural start to my day. Unfortunately, once I had loaded up, there wasn't much time to eat the most important meal of the day. Away we went to Old Jaffa, the Arab town on which Tel Aviv was built, and then to the home studio of an allegedly famous but not very talented artist, then to a wine bar, then a quick tour through a renovated neighbourhood, then lunch at Kyoto Salsa, a Tex-Mex sushi bar, then to Rothschild Boulevard to see the architecture and meet Etgar Keret at a sidewalk café.

Sarah had suggested I interview the Israeli writer, and her judgment was spot on. Keret, I'd found as I sped through two of his books on the plane, was a terrific writer of microscopically short stories. In just four paragraphs he manages to be both ribald and poignant, a mix that I wanted to think was uniquely Israeli. As we waited for him at the café, I flipped through *The Nimrod Flipout* to come up with a few questions. I fell upon "Halibut," a story about two Israelis at a seaside restaurant, one dissatisfied with his "smelly, sad, dull" country, the other his irritated friend, who's offended that the news of his engage-ment isn't getting more of a reaction. Oh, and the glum Israeli becomes even more so when the talking fish he orders doesn't talk to him. As I wondered whether the restaurant in the story was the same one we'd eaten at the night before, Keret arrived.

Without too much prompting, he began to explain the country in terms that Nurit would never use.

"In Israel," he said, "there's something obnoxious in the infrastructure. It's life at full volume. Everything is out front. Every town has a sewer system, but here it's in the street."

Was this, I wondered, the Larry David ideal, a society that by necessity had done away with niceties that didn't make sense?

"America is a very repressed society," Keret said. "On the west coast, they hug you without touching you. I said to my friend there, 'Women here have a way of hugging you so you can't touch their boobs.'"

The ultimate Israeli experience, Keret told us, was a cab ride.

"You get in and say, 'Start the meter.' The driver says, 'Why, you asshole?' Then he offers you some of his food and by the end of the trip, he asks you to marry his daughter."

Sarah laughed at this, but Keret explained that Israelis wouldn't see the humour in such a situation.

"Humour is a Jewish trait, but it's not an Israeli one," he said. "Humour is a form of empathy. It's the weapon of the weak, a way of forming a protest without being pathetic. In many ways, Israelis are the opposite of Diaspora Jews. Jews are the people of the book; Israelis have the most powerful army in the world. Jewish writers, like Philip Roth, don't sell here. Jewish food doesn't sell here. There's a joke that when you go for

Jewish food, five minutes after you order, a Cossack will come and throw up on your table and rape your wife."

During this interview, Nurit asked a few questions about stories she hadn't read, but didn't contradict any of his points. I filled half a notebook with Keret's answers, and it was only on our ride back to the hotel that I began to consider what he'd said. I had thought of the Jewish homeland as a place where I'd find a concentrated version of the culture I knew, but in fact it was something very different. I didn't have time to discuss this idea with Sarah as we were rushed to our room to freshen up for our dinner with the Gordon Ramsay of Israel. By the end of day two, we were floored. The pace only seemed to escalate after that.

The next day, we went north to Caesarea, a dusty historical site that had been ill-advisedly turned into a Biblical theme park. It may have been the perfect combination of elements to create a place that Sarah and I would never, ever choose to visit.

By lunchtime, we began to suspect that Ehad was more than a driver. If he wasn't behind the wheel, he seemed to be by our side. When Sarah tired of listening to Nurit's history lessons, she tried to talk to Ehad, with limited success.

"So, Ehad, do you have a girlfriend?"

"No."

"Are you looking for a girlfriend?"

"Yes."

"What kind of women do you like?"

"All kinds."

We returned to Nurit's dull recap of what the Romans did to the Jews at Caesarea.

After the meal, it was on to several vineyard tours on

which the ratio of touring to tasting was suboptimal, then another town, then an artists' village, then Haifa. Many of these sites would have been nice places to spend an afternoon, but we didn't have that kind of time. Nurit was indefatigable, displaying the enthusiasm of someone crossing items off her to-do list. Sensory overload kicked in early, primarily induced by the talking King Herod animations at Caesarea. By the time we arrived at our hotel in Haifa, I was a zombie tourist.

"And I liked Haifa," I later told Sarah, which was true. Though our breakneck schedule required us to be in and out of the city in under twelve hours, it was just long enough to experience something we hadn't yet encountered in the country: a normal, tourist-free, low-tension place.

That night, in our only unscripted social visit of the trip—and come to think of it, we may have been tailed by Ehad—we visited Dov, Benny and Nomi, Jake's cousins who lived in the hills surrounding the city. Benny and Nomi's bungalow reminded me of the houses of Sarah's California relatives. More important, it was a home. Benny talked about how his dentistry practice slowed to nothing during the war with Lebanon, when missile attacks shut down the city. He spoke fondly of his children, asked about Sarah's sisters, poured Scotch and paused to remember when Sarah had first come to Israel as a teenager. When a young Sarah had been bedridden by a nasty intestinal bug, her cousin Foofie—a perfectly normal Israeli diminutive, she assured me—had brought her the complete *Calvin and Hobbes* collection. Sarah was comfortable here, and by proxy I was, too. Sitting in the recessed living room with a glass of Johnnie Walker Green Label—much better than the red or black, I learned on that trip—I began to realize that if I was converting to Judaism to solidify my status in Sarah's family, it was not only unnecessary but inefficient. Spending actual time with her family made more sense. (It certainly made more sense than spending time at Biblical theme parks.) Religion was an important bond in theory, but much less so in practice. It was more important just to be there. And we were there for a few short hours, before our travels caught up with us and we started to fall asleep. Dov drove us back to the hotel.

Breakfast the next morning was another rushed affair and a reminder that, aside from the night before, every single scheduled minute fell under the watchful eye of Nurit. She was apparently obligated to see every sight, eat every meal and spend every waking hour with us. She was quite terrified by the tourism ministry—and to be fair, hearing her side of cellphone conversations with them helped us understand her fearfulness. It seemed as though she would be personally held to account if we fell behind in our schedule, even in the slightest. That afternoon, as we started to feel ground down by the passing parade of antiquities, we reasoned with her: "Please don't make us go horseback riding this afternoon! We know it's on the schedule, and we're thankful that someone organized it, but neither of us has any desire to ride horses! We would be much happier reading by the hotel pool." That was the only victory we won in our week with Nurit.

One thing my mother had warned me about before our trip was how small everything was. When she'd sat in church as a child and heard stories of Jesus at the Sea of Galilee, she'd pictured a bona fide sea. When she saw it, she said, she was surprised that it was no bigger than Otter Lake. (This comment, with its incredulous comparison of the Bible lands to eastern Ontario's cottage country, was repeated constantly.) The town itself was no more or less impressive than any past-its-prime seaside resort.

We dined at the Chinese restaurant that night—the same one, we'd learn, that everyone passing through Galilee on a Friday night visits. It was at that meal that we officially ran out of subjects to discuss with Nurit. Faced with the prospect of two hours of listening to each other chew, when the won ton soup was done and the rest of the meal seemed an eternity away, I had no choice but to ask: "So, Nurit, what's your opinion of the situation with the Palestinians?" It was a tedious recap of modern Israeli history, but it got us through to the fortune cookies.

The culmination of our trip was Jerusalem. We arrived after a long drive through the desert, with Sarah and me waking up in the back of the hot van. It took me a moment to realize where we were and that my contact lenses were now glued to my eyes. My first glimpses of the world's holiest city were through those dirty bits of plastic, so I can't blame the city for looking dusty and parched. The next thing I noticed were the security guards everywhere. I was initially surprised by the orange-vested retirees at the doors of the occasional shop in Tel Aviv—back home, the equivalent job would be a greeter at Walmart, which for all its faults is much less risky. In Jerusalem, they were omnipresent and represented by every age and ethnic group. This sudden increase in police presence may have made ne'er-do-wells think twice, but it made me much less comfortable. I thought of an article I had read on the plane about Jerusalem syndrome, a condition in which previously normal people become psychotic upon arriving in the city, delivering sermons, destroying land-marks from competing religions, performing miracles and gen-erally raising hell while trying to do the opposite. The gist of the article had been that Israeli officials were now well trained in spotting this sort of behaviour before the average Joe tried to walk on water. As I looked around, I became increasingly unconvinced. There were plenty of religious tourists on view, all weird in their own ways. Between davening, swaying in prayer, mouthing silent devotions and simply looking around agog and in awe, how could you possibly tell who was nuts and who was devout?

A visit to the Western Wall is supposed to be a visit to the holiest of Jewish landmarks. It's the last remaining piece of the Second Temple, and the reason Orthodox synagogues don't call themselves by the T-word. As luck—or religious tri-umphalism—would have it, Muhammad chose that exact spot to ascend to heaven, hence the presence of the Dome of the Rock, the third-holiest site in Islam, directly on top of the Temple grounds. You might think one religion's holiest site would trump another's third-holiest, but to think that way is to apply logic to the most illogical of human activities. Instead, it's best simply to be impressed that the whole thing has stayed relatively intact—with the occasional minor bombing—despite being constantly surrounded by religious fanatics.

Slipping a written prayer between the cracks of the wall sounded more silly than spiritual to me, but Sarah, Nurit and I had gone through intense security to get here, so I went ahead with it. To keep Orthodox Jews happy, men and women visit different portions of the wall. I walked up alone, having a sudden fear that, as I was no longer Christian and not yet a Jew, I didn't belong there. There were people waiting in line, after all, and I was just a tourist. I scribbled my prayer down and began my approach. I can't honestly recall what I wrote—something about keeping family and friends safe perhaps, likely in response to all the machine guns on display in the vicinity—but then, I'm not sure that I'm supposed to reveal my prayer. In this respect, the whole affair seems more like a birthday wish than the petitioning of a higher power. As I neared the wall, a young Orthodox Jew with a scraggly beard approached me.

"Are you Jewish?" he asked in a thick accent.

"Almost," I said.

"Please come with me, then."

"I'm not Jewish yet, though! I mean, I can't complete a *minyan!*"

I followed him, thinking I might be the target of a scam, but what kind of Orthodox Jew would do something like that on the holiest site in Judaism?

He walked quickly to the left side of the wall, weaving through the pilgrims and motioning for me to keep up. He ducked into a door at the far side of the area, and against my better judgment I followed him. Inside was what looked like a library. The stone walls were dramatically lit, and I realized I was the only person in the room not wearing a beard. At that point, the man who had signalled me in began showing me pamphlets and, in a voice too hushed and hurried to fully understand, telling me what the function of this room was. As soon as I made out the words "your donation," my natural reaction to solicitation kicked in, better late than never.

"Thank you very much, but I'm not interested!" I said, too loudly for the chamber, as I hurried back toward the door.

I returned to the wall, took a deep breath and stuffed my prayer into a crack that was already bulging with notes. I should have been focused on the prayer, but instead I was trying to figure out what had just happened. Wasn't that proselytizing? No, I had said I was *almost* Jewish, and he was just after a few shekels. More importantly, why had I let my guard down in this city of religious excess? Despite my hesitation, I was hoping for a resonant experience at the Wall—not the Jerusalem syndrome, but just a tiny shiver. I was still determined to embrace this religion on purely logical grounds, but a bit of emotion would have been nice. In Jerusalem, I began to admit the possibility that the truly devout might know—or more accurately, feel—something I didn't. I bitterly concluded that the main thing this observant Jew knew was how to shake down a wide-eyed tourist for some yeshiva funding.

"I know it's a horrible thing to say, but I have to say it," I told Sarah. "I really didn't like Jerusalem at all."

"So, the first five hours of Tel Aviv and a dinner in Haifa were the only parts of the trip you enjoyed? That's less than half a day of a week-long trip, and on the rest of it you were complaining."

"So were you! And with good reason. This schedule was nuts and the guide was irritating."

"I know it's frustrating, but you have to separate the guide and the touristy stuff from the country itself. My dad was born here, and I feel strangely at home here. Actually, it's not strange: Jews feel at home here. Israelis are different, but they're still Jews. Eventually, you'll feel at home here."

"I'll try to be open-minded, but I can't imagine that."

Our exchange of goodbyes with Nurit was curt and perfunctory, though that was her usual demeanour. We didn't exchange email addresses or volunteer to keep in touch, though there were awkward full-contact hugs.

It was a relief to get back onto Canadian soil. I knew I was going to have to give Jake a rundown of the trip. "Life-changing!" would be a perfect reaction. "Aggravating!" would not. To avoid drawing it out, I sent him an email as soon as we'd unpacked, CC'ing Sarah.

I titled it "Errett's Israel," a frankly terrific pun on the Hebrew word "*eretz,*" or "land of." I opted for convenient list form.

1. *Tel Aviv = (Miami + Paris)/2 + many more Jews.* That was fairly positive, I reasoned.

2. *Why go to the Dead Sea if you're not going to go in the Dead Sea?* This stop was unambiguously my favourite part of the trip. The sheer fun of slathering yourself in mud, walking down a desert road and plunging into an otherworldly salt lake was hard to resist. But at first it seemed like it would be a disappointment, as tour bus after tour bus full of pasty Russians filled the entrance hall and the sulphur pools. Once we had changed and walked down to the actual Dead Sea, we were practically on our own. These tourists had come all the way to one of the world's natural wonders and opted to stop thirty feet short of their destination.

3. *Will the kosher not watch cooking shows because they're afraid they might see a shrimp?* That thought stemmed from our dinner

with the aforementioned Israeli Gordon Ramsay—though he looked more like the Jewish Jamie Oliver. He had offhandedly mocked the religiously observant who would not watch his shows.

4. *Should we have told native Hebrew speakers that the plural of shrimp is not shrimps?* Cheap shot!

5. *Sushi with cheese? Really?* Kyoto Salsa hadn't sat well.

6. *How is it that a country of six million people, in which English is a second language, has not one but two quality English daily newspapers?* Specifically, *Haaretz* and the *Jerusalem Post,* though the former was clearly better. When we weren't asleep in the back of the minivan, we passed the time on the road reading the complimentary papers until we got carsick.

7. *I think our driver was a Mossad agent.* The more I think about it, the more I'm sure of it.

8. *I'm glad we don't have intifadas here.* Enough said.

9. *This whole Kabbalah thing? Not convinced.* After Haifa, we'd stopped in Sefad, the home of Jewish mysticism, and were shown around by a nice but nutty devotee of the faith. He assured us that Madonna and Ashton Kutcher don't present the true nature of Kabbalism, but after a two-hour tour of the village, I don't think he did, either.

10. *Mandatory military service really changes the character of a nation.* Everyone we met referred to their time in the army, staffing checkpoints or doing technical work or drills in the desert. At the beginning of the trip, I thought it was terrible that the country was under such constant threat that they all had to serve in the military. By the end, I began to think it wouldn't be so bad if we had the same requirement back home. Why let your most able-bodied citizens spend all their time drinking and warding off quarter-life crises? On the other hand, why put them in harm's way before they've begun their lives?

Jake responded in point form.

1. plus 10% new york
2. going into dead sea is mandatory
3. no
4. no. i say shrimps sometimes.
5. sushi rolls here often have cream cheese in them
6. old joke: if you have two jews, you get three opinions. same applies to newspapers.
7. doubt it
8. me too
9. me too
10. always regretted not serving when they detained me in israel

(He was born there but was raised almost entirely in Canada, which led to some tricky questions from security on his first voyage back.)

To all others who asked how the trip was, I simply said it was intense. I rehashed my parsings with Sarah, but couldn't get the ratio of time I'd actually enjoyed to more than a tenth of our visit. This was a hard fact to ignore, or to ascribe to a hatred of tourist traps, and it annoyed Sarah for reasons she couldn't fully explain. Most of my complaints were valid, she admitted, but she still hoped I would have had a more positive view. If I didn't feel at home in the homeland of the Jews, how could I become a Jew?

רְמִידִיאַל
הִיבְּרוּ

Remedial Hebrew

Yofi tofi is the Hebrew equivalent of "okey-dokey," and by this point I thought it described my linguistic progress. My trip to Israel was like a week of immersion, I figured. No less an authority than my mother backed me up on this, suggesting that I even deserved extra credit in class for my pilgrimage. (Ruth simply marked us absent for two weeks.) But what the trip taught me was that the Hebrew in the prayer books is quite different from the Hebrew spoken in Israel. As Nurit told us, the founders of Israel needed a common tongue to make the desert bloom. The European Ashkenazi Jews spoke Yiddish, while the Middle Eastern Sephardic Jews spoke Ladino, a close cousin of Spanish. They all read Hebrew in their prayer books, so it was decided that the holy written language would become the word on the streets. This, she told us, was the only time in history that an all-but-dead language was resurrected and used to found a nation. In the process, all sorts of words that never came up in the Torah had to be coined, as no one ever received a text message in the days of the Temple.

To further complicate things, none of these words had vowels. In class, we learned that word sounds changed based on where the little dots around them hovered. The first letter we learned was aleph, which looks like this: א

Ruth was adamant that we match the shape of the letter to the sounds, not to the letters of the English alphabet they might resemble. Aleph by itself has no sound, so Ruth—in her purple sweatsuit—struck a jumping jack with pursed lips. That, she said, would help us remember the silent letter. Then we learned it has a vowel that sometimes accompanies it, as follows:

א The horizontal line was like a tongue depressor, which is why it makes the sound "aaaah." Ruth stuck out her tongue while she told us this. Again, it was memorable. Then there were more vowels, each with an accompanying mnemonic.

א Look, there's a little mouse running by silent Ruth doing a jumping-jack! That makes her shriek—"Eeeee!"

א This, she told us, was the Canadian vowel, which is pronounced "eh."

That led her to the American vowel (א), which gets an "eh" as in "meh!" "That's what we think of those Americans with their wars. Meh!" (Sarah found this needlessly insulting, and I couldn't disagree.)

In Israel, and in real-world Hebrew, the dots are dusted away and you just know the correct sound from context. I knew this would be difficult to get the hang of when the marks were described to me as training wheels, the mention of which reminded me of the time my dear mother, frustrated with what she saw as my unnecessary clinging to the transitional bike, put me on a two-wheeler and pushed me down a grassy hill. To be fair, I've often been back to that spot in Westmount Park and the hill is more of a gentle slope, but at the time it was steep enough. I clearly remember that this event took place on Easter—perhaps, on a subconscious level, that was the beginning of my disenfranchisement with Christianity. While her efforts eventually got me cycling, the most immediate result was to make me really appreciate my training wheels.

Israel, with its grown-up, freewheeling Hebrew written all over the place, had the opposite effect. Enough of these silly reading circles; this is the big time! Of course, I didn't actually need to read anything, so every word I could sound out was merely a bonus. I became proficient at making lightly educated guesses at what various words sounded like, and because many of the stores and signs there had English words transliterated into Hebrew, there was some gratification when I cracked the code.

"BLAH!

"BLAH-CH!

"BLACH-BOOS!

"BLACH-BOOSTER!

"Blockbuster!"

"Good for you!" Sarah said with enthusiasm. "You're really getting the hang of this!"

"Well," I replied, trying to stay humble despite my obvious knack for the language, "it helped that the sign had yellow block letters on a blue background and was on top of a video store."

Similarly, I could read the words "Tel Aviv" on the side of municipal garbage trucks and, by looking only at the Hebrew letters, deduce that the national airline was called El Al. You wouldn't think that could fool anyone, but I let myself be lulled into thinking I was, if not at the head of the class, at least among the best of the newbies.

I was distracted enough by the mouthing of these guttural sounds that I didn't dwell on the fact that it was no way to make sense of a language. The goal was to be able to sing along with the prayers, not understand what you were actually intoning. Only rarely would we learn what words actually meant. Pedagogically, this was logical: you have to crawl in Hebrew before you can walk. Still, I found it slightly disconcerting that actual comprehension of the language of the Jews was too remote a prospect for us to consider. Shouldn't we allocate as much time to the content of the prayers as their form? Since I had difficulty telling my *het* from my *mem,* I didn't dare raise the point.

Ten minutes of practice a day would make us Hebrew All-Stars, Ruth said. It ended up being more like half an hour the night before the class, plus an extra twenty minutes on the commute. Our Monday night homework would be done at the kitchen table, where Sarah would follow the text with her finger as we read together. When she was on an illustration deadline, we'd relocate upstairs to her office, where I would stumble through the prayerbook as she drew until she asked me to try a word again.

We seemed to be on par with our peers. The gentile halves of each couple were all making slow and steady progress, though it was still a colossal exercise in patience for the Jews, who had been taught this stuff as children and now, because they had chosen to become romantically involved with a well-meaning goy, had to sit though it again. To ramp up the ennui, Ruth employed all those irritating teacher strategies we'd thought we'd all left behind: the breaking up into groups to work with each other, going around the room to read aloud in turns, and sneaking up on our reading circles to pass judgment on each student.

When we went around the room reading, the class divisions became horribly evident. If it was me or one of my fellow beginners, we'd count ahead to guess which line we had to read, then puzzle out as much of it as we could. As we were reading out of prayer books, the words *Baruch ata Adonai*—Blessed are You our God—came up all the time. They were like spinning the wheel and getting a free turn.

"Remember, you're going for accuracy, not speed," Ruth would say if one of us tried unsuccessfully to read at a normal pace. That was easy for her to say. We stressed-out Hebrew novices had only to look over at our partners, yawning, staring out the window or, in Sarah's case, doodling in her sketchbook, to know we were dragging things out.

When it came time for Sarah or her experienced Jewish peers to read, they looked up from their sketchbooks, rattled off a string of words faster than we gentiles could follow along with our fingers on the page and got right back to looking bored.

Our first class after returning from Israel featured a reading circle in which I became the focus of Ruth's attention. At that point, any delusions that I was keeping up were quickly done away with. I stumbled through a prayer and, sensing her disapproval, became nervous and made more mistakes. She didn't let me end my turn, but instead made me go over the line again and again until I got it.

"El-ee-dah . . ."

"One more time."

"El-ee-ha . . ."

"Again."

"El-ee-heh vey . . ."

"Again."

"El-ee-heh Ne-tsor Le Sev . . ."

"Try that again."

"Le Shev . . ."

And that was just three words; she made me recite at least ten before deducing that perhaps my comfort level with the language was lacking.

"You really have to practise," she admonished.

"I am," I said, counting the trip to Israel as practice. "All last week I practised."

Sarah was working in a different group, and I heard Ruth take her aside. She spoke in a stage whisper, presumably for maximum shaming effect.

"I'm worried about him!" Ruth hissed. "He's not keeping up! Is he practising?"

"Yes, we practise," Sarah replied. "He was so good last week in Israel!"

"You have to practise with him! He's really falling behind."

They both looked over at me, as did everyone else in the class. Up until this moment, I hadn't really considered the possibility that I might not ace the course. My academic days were well behind me, but surely I still had what it took. A return to the elementary-school classroom would, at worst, be slightly dull. Now, though, I wasn't bored. I felt myself blushing with both embarrassment and anger. I'd somewhat snobbishly assumed I wouldn't have to work very hard, and now I was being called out on it.

Even the native speakers snapped out of their daydreams for a moment to see who was in danger of flunking the language they could speak so fluently. Time ground to a halt. The other groups stopped practising and turned to watch me. Even the fluorescent lights stopped buzzing.

At that moment, I was sorely tempted to gather my belongings and leave the classroom. All the students who had seen me roll my eyes and heard me complain about the child-like pace of the class were now seeing me fail to meet these low expectations. But hold on: I wasn't a bad student! This whole system was out of order! I didn't need to put up with this. In that second, I imagined channelling my humiliation into an epic rant.

"I'm very sorry if your teaching methods haven't turned me into a fluent Talmudic scholar yet, Ruth," I would growl through clenched teeth. "Like everyone else in this room, with the possible exception of you, I'm quite busy during the day. I practise this as often as I can and spend the cab rides here each week cramming. And you know what? I can muddle through fairly well when you aren't looking down your nose at me."

All right, I didn't really hate her that much, but it felt good to entertain the possibility of such an outburst. Surely this was what Susan and Ari were thinking, too. I continued the dark fantasy.

"And another thing, Ruth: while I may not appreciate your teaching style, I make every effort to get here every week and listen to your inane, irrelevant stories that teach me little to nothing about this beautiful religion. Why do I do this? I'm making this effort for myself, for Sarah and for the religion, but I'm not making it for you. To be perfectly honest, you're just another obstacle. And that's just sad, because it doesn't have to be this way! You could inspire and enlighten us. But you choose instead to bore us to tears and—when it pleases you, or perhaps when even you are stupefied by your own inane stories—to humiliate those of us who are trying their best to keep up."

She would stand there slack-jawed, and the looks of pity I was getting from my classmates would turn to looks of awe. I would be like Jack Nicholson in *A Few Good Men*. Now to reach the stirring conclusion and clinch my Academy Award.

"Well, with all due respect, ma'am"—this would be said in a mocking tone to make clear that no respect was due— "I've had enough. I'd like to walk out of this classroom and forget I ever thought about taking this class, but I'm not going to give you the satisfaction. I'm not the only one who feels this way. In fact, I think I'm in the majority. And since majority rules, I demand you show the hard-working students here some respect. From now on, no one gets humiliated or shushed. From now on, we're in this together, in an atmosphere of civility and respect. From now on, we stick to the curriculum and avoid wasting time with useless anecdotes. I'll practise, all right, but only if that's the kind of class I'm practising for!"

I would be standing on my chair at the end of that speech, which even in my imagination wasn't as dramatic as it sounds, since we were in a children's classroom. A slow clap from one of my fellow potential converts would break the room's silence. Then another pair of hands would join in, and another, and soon the whole classroom would have erupted into thunderous applause.

This instant catharsis helped as I listened to Ruth rat me out to Sarah. If nothing else, it prevented me from storming out. Somehow, eventually, the class ended. My relief was temporary, and by the time we were on the bus it had mutated into resentment. Sarah could see the black cloud hovering over my head.

"It's okay. You'll practise some more and get it down cold."

"I don't know if I even want to anymore," I said melodramatically. "I don't want to give her the satisfaction."

"It's not about her! It's about you, and us. You set out to do this, and you're going to let *her* stop you?"

"Maybe I will."

"She's ridiculous, but now you're being ridiculous, too."

"*You've* got to help me," I said, redirecting my frustration. "We're supposed to be in this together, but it's more like me cramming and you half-listening. No wonder I can't get it."

"You know I've always been supportive," Sarah replied, irritated.

"Yeah, but your version of being supportive is telling me I'm doing a great job after five minutes of practice, then I walk in there and get blown out of the water. How is that supportive?"

Sarah looked crushed and said nothing. I realized I had dumped all my frustration on her simply because I could, which only made me feel worse. We sat in silence for the rest of the bus ride, then transferred to the subway, rode one stop, walked the three blocks home and climbed the front steps before I said something.

"You *have* been supportive. Of course you have. I'm sorry."

"It's okay, I know you were upset," Sarah said, and I could see that her eyes were slightly wet.

"But I don't need to take it out on you. I'm an idiot."

"I'll help you. We'll work harder."

"No, *I'll* work harder. I keep saying we're in this together, but that's not supposed to be a way to blame us instead of me."

I realized then that all of my metaphysical fears that this was too easy and not engaging enough were a bit rich, coming from a man who wasn't doing his homework. In other words, it was time to put that whole "action over belief" thing into action.

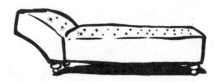

A Second Opinion

As I considered my struggle with Hebrew, I realized my natural ineptitude with second languages didn't help my cause. Admittedly, this realization was a convenient way to blame something other than my lack of practice. The record did back me up, though: I had been sent to an all-French Catholic school in Montreal from kindergarten to grade three and had taken French classes sporadically thereafter. When we moved to the States, Spanish was on the curriculum, which led to a damaging mismatch of romance languages. So, despite the fact that my maternal grandmother was still more comfortable in French and I had spent my university years in the world's second-largest francophone city, I could still only produce a heavily accented and mispronounced version of Molière's language.

I told all this to my grandmother Laurette when she asked how the conversion was going, as if the language was the only thing that stood in my way. She quickly moved the conversation along to a more pressing issue: the timing and location of the wedding. We'd left things unresolved since our tour of Boca Raton's finest hotels four months before, a state of affairs that didn't worry us but clearly annoyed my nan.

"Look, why don't youse"—she always pluralized the pronoun, a carryover from French—"just have the wedding in Montreal? It'll be easy for us to get there on the train and the traffic won't be as bad as in Toronto." (This was always a concern with all my Smiths Falls relatives, who assumed that traffic and violent crime were the big city's leading industries.)

Nan had given orders all her life—and they were orders, not suggestions—usually to her children. To my surprise, I found this one quite useful.

"That's actually a very good idea," I told her.

"Your mother will be close, so she can help. And I'm sure *he* can find a good place for youse to have the ceremony."

"He," when spoken by my grandmother in reference to my mother, was The Professor, my mother's longtime gentleman friend and a respected professor of engineering at McGill. Both he and my grandmother are very set in their ways, a state of affairs that had nearly pushed my mother over the edge when the three of them had set out to drive Laurette's white Cadillac from Fort Lauderdale back to Smiths Falls. Nan, who had handled the drive for a quarter-century, knew exactly which restaurants, motels and rest stops she liked. She also knew that listening to Elton John's tribute to Princess Diana relaxed her.

The Professor liked to mark happy hour at a certain time of the afternoon and liked a hot mug of tea at another specific time later in the evening. When he saw a fruit stand by the side of the road, he demanded they stop to purchase a dozen white grapefruits. He would proceed to bring this produce into restaurants and ask to have it served with his meal.

There was little overlap in their schedules and little room for compromise. As well, Nan liked to be on the road by 6:15 each day; at this exact time, The Professor liked to head out for a run, then enjoy several strong cups of tea, one of his grapefruits and perhaps a Weetabix. When they finally arrived in Washington, my mother had had enough of the bickering. She tried to put him on a plane back to Montreal, but he refused. As a compromise, she bought him the Sunday *New York Times,* which he read in the back seat while drinking a bottle of wine. Up front, Nan tuned him out with the help of Elton. Eventually, my mother got them both back to her house in Vermont, where The Professor's car awaited.

The lasting result of this trip was Nan's refusal to speak his name; they got along just fine, but it was always, "Will *he* be there?" And he *would* be there, thankfully. My mother was on side with the Montreal venue and volunteered The Professor's backyard for a garden party. The Professor was initially surprised by the idea, but she assured me it wouldn't be a problem. Indeed, he was happy to host such an event.

Once we had The Professor on board, the venue was obvious: the university's faculty club. As a past president of the wood-panelled sanctuary for the tenured, The Professor knew the lay of the land. As a student, I had rarely been granted access to the domain of the professorial class, though I knew it to be stuffed with portraits of the university's mutton-chopped founders. When Sarah and I arranged a lunch there with The Professor and my mother, we also found they cooked the salmon to a paste-like consistency, perhaps to the liking of the academic set. Still, it looked like the mansion from the board game Clue and—assuming those bankrolling the whole operation were on side—it was perfect.

Jacob Lazarovic, a man who is particular in his own way, did his best to adjust to this sudden change in our plans. "This was unexpected," he wrote in a terse email. "But I'm sure it will work out. What do you know about the quality of the food/service there?" We didn't mention the salmon and agreed to set up a tasting trip. This was all the notice Debbie needed to swing into action, researching florists, photographers, hotels and wedding bands. We booked our train and hoped for the best.

Around this time, I was having a somewhat unexpected bout of career anxiety. I knew that on some level my medical-school refusal would always tempt me to consider what might have been, but those thoughts were usually only triggered by setbacks of some sort. Sure, there was the long-term decline of the printed newspaper to be concerned about, as well as the bank's continued gratitude for my biweekly mortgage payments. This was different, though. This wasn't about money or status or the repressed desire to save lives instead of editing crossword puzzles; it was existential. This was about realizing that it wasn't too late, yet, but that it eventually would be. I casually jotted down the names of med-school references I could likely still call; the many years away from my undergraduate biology studies could perhaps be justified in a creative way.

Sarah offered her cautious support for whatever I wanted to do. The number of slashes necessary to describe her career as an illustrator/cartoonist/filmmaker/animator/webmistress/writer/etc. often irritated her, so she understood the motivation to define oneself more clearly. My mother was more blunt when I confided my thoughts to her. "I think that's a horrible idea," she said. "You've got a job you enjoy and are good at. Why would you leave that to become a doctor?" As a nurse, she had developed a life-long hatred of MDs. An acrimonious divorce from one didn't help matters. As for my father, well, now that our relationship was approaching something that resembled normalcy, I wasn't about to throw this semi-considered plan into the mix.

I was turning the matter over in my mind that weekend as we visited the florist.

We decided to skip the elaborate centrepieces in favour of a few petals spread on each table. I wondered if it would be possible to start at McGill med that fall. We met with the photographer, a staffer from *The Gazette* whose experience covering breaking news more than equipped him for our big day. I considered renting out our house in Toronto in anticipation of my return to Montreal. In this hypothetical scenario, I'd also finally learn French. I was less than helpful during our wedding planning weekend.

Not that I needed to offer much support: Debbie had the whole thing under control to the point that she even found time to buy me the second and third instalments of *The Jewish Catalog*, a hippied-out reference for the groovily devout. She pledged to keep looking for the first; I assured her that wasn't necessary.

On Sunday morning, Sarah and I were having coffee with my old friend Ryan and his wife, Marie, while waiting for Jake and Debbie to arrive for the second day of our planning weekend. In our time together as college roommates, Ryan and I had not only learned about existentialism and Buddhism, we had also both met our future wives and consequently were each the other couple's closest pair of friends. Marie was a Parisian exchange student who had come to Canada in part because of a dare with friends. Their life in Paris had become dull, and whoever could make the biggest break from it would win their bet.

"When I met Ryan, this guy from Saskatchewan who smoked a pipe and had a woodstove in his apartment, I knew I had won," she explained. It didn't sound like the strongest foundation for a marriage, but then, Marie had a tendency to exaggerate for dramatic effect.

They got married a year after graduating, and we happily attended both the wedding held in his hometown of Prince Albert, Saskatchewan, and the ceremony held a year later at her family's property in Corsica. Sheaves of wheat and branches of olives were the centrepieces at each table at both weddings, symbolizing the glorious clash of cultures.

Ryan had built a successful legal career on his own in Montreal, and Marie's Parisian sophistication served her well in a marketing job at a French cosmetic company's Canadian head office. They married well before us, but we beat them on the house by two years. After they bought, Ryan joked that he had considered putting a down payment on a cemetery plot as well, just to end any competition between us once and for all. The greatest irritant in our friendship was Paulette, their highly

BENJAMIN ERRETT

allergenic cat, but Sarah would gladly spend a weekend doped up on antihistamines for our friends.

Ryan had undergone a religious awakening in his teens, going so far as to be baptized in the Ukrainian Orthodox church of his elders. He embraced Catholicism to marry Marie, and while he openly admitted a cultural and historic attachment to religion, he wasn't exactly a believer. Still, he would never pass up an opportunity to tease me about leaving Christianity behind.

"So, can you feel Jesus Christ clawing his way back into your heart, Ben?" Ryan asked after I noticed that his crucifix with footrests, which I'd commented upon back in university, was now hanging in their kitchen.

"Jesus who?" I asked. "To me, he's just another historical figure now."

"Oh, come now," Ryan teased. "His love is everywhere! Don't deny it."

"That's like saying Alexander the Great's love is everywhere. He's been dead for thousands of years. Nice try, though."

Meanwhile, Sarah was filling Marie in on our Passover trip, seeds of information that would find fertile ground in her mind. As Ryan would lovingly say of his wife, "Her stories aren't always the literal truth, but in a way, though they're often apocryphal, they get at a larger truth that we might not even have known at the time." This was yet another way his philosophy degree was put to daily use. The truth Marie chose to extrapolate from Sarah's update was that my mysterious conversion—a decision that, clearly, I'd *still* never adequately explained to anyone—was being undertaken to please Aunt Sandy. I didn't

136

hear this theory on that day, but subsequent research has pin-pointed it as the rumour's ground zero.

Having dispelled the idea that I had a secret urge to return to the church, I told Ryan about the larger issue on my mind. He listened attentively, and perhaps as a lawyerly course of habit asked a series of probing questions before forming his response. Could I be readmitted based on my previous applica-tion? Would I need to retake the MCAT? What did Sarah think about returning to Montreal? We were in the middle of this inquisition when Jake arrived. As he and Debbie had split up to get all the day's chores done twice as fast, he was charged with collecting the future bride and groom.

"So, gang," Jake asked after disdainfully shooing the cat off a chair. "What's the POA?" I realized he meant the plan of attack for the day, not my career, but I decided to present the dilemma anyway. Jake was, and is, a doctor, trained at McGill. He is the chief medical officer for a company that handles work-er's compensation claims, though according to his daughter he has long dreamed of a second career as a travel writer. He was also my future father-in-law. Stability and success for his daugh-ter's family would be paramount for him, I was sure. I realized I had bought into the stereotype of the Jewish parent. Don't they always want their children to be doctors? What other profession combines such prestige and such income?

"Well," I began, "we were just discussing my crazy plan to go to medical school." He gave me a quizzical look.

"Is this a new crazy plan?"

"Relatively new, yeah."

"What brought it on?"

"To be honest, I'm not really sure. I just realized that I'm still young and it's something I could easily do."

"It's not exactly easy. It's at least four years to begin, and then a residency of three to five years to specialize—"

"Okay, maybe 'easy' was the wrong word. It's something I could possibly do, I'll say."

"But you could possibly do anything. Why would it be this?"

"Um, good question." By this point, I had laid myself down on the couch, a position that Ryan later pointed out was ideal for this sort of psychoanalysis.

"I guess I had this opportunity once and can envision having it again."

"That's kind of a silly reason. You and Sarah have all sorts of terrific opportunities, of which this is just one. Do you actually want to practise medicine?"

"I suppose it would be fulfilling."

"I know a lot of doctors who don't find it fulfilling at all. There are too many patients and not enough time, so it's a daily challenge to live up to your professional obligations. And the hours can be ridiculous."

"I remember that growing up, as I didn't see my dad much until I was a teenager."

"There are definite benefits to the profession, which I'm sure you're aware of, but you should consider the drawbacks as well. Do you have a real desire to help the sick?"

"Honestly? Not really."

"Then I'd have to say this probably isn't the best idea for you. But it's not a binary choice; you can still do anything you want. Look at my daughter," he said as he squeezed her nose. "She has at least three careers at any one time, and those are only the ones she tells us about."

This conversation was unexpected, and all the more powerful for it. My daydreams about a career change were just that, substitutions of an ideal, problem-free world for the real and not-too-shabby one in front of me. Jake didn't really tell me anything I didn't already know, but he made me actually work it out and see that there were several million other professional options in front of me.

After I figured this out, I felt a bit guilty for not seeking this guidance from my own father. This was paternal advice, it seemed, and while I was glad to have more of it, I had no right to complain about not getting it from my dad if I never solicited it. But then I considered Jake's counsel to his own daughters, a never-ending series of questions, comments, concerns and suggestions that prompted reactions ranging from eye-rolls to complete exasperation from Sarah, Becky and Jane. This was an occupational hazard of parenthood, I realized. Maybe you can't give objective life advice to someone you spent twenty years raising. Maybe, in the grand design of things, that's what in-laws were for. And maybe I should cut my own parents a bit more slack.

The Fun out of Funerals

My renewed determination to embrace my Jewish studies coincided with death, or rather our class on that subject. As morbid as it sounds, I was actually predisposed to enjoy this lecture. In addition to the suitably respectful and cathartic funerals I'd attended, we had learned that the Jews were deliberately vague on what came afterward. This, I'd realized, had bothered me about religion ever since I'd been told that all dogs do not go to heaven: who are these people who think they know what happens after we shuffle off this mortal coil?

Religion's all well and good when it tells us how to behave on Earth, but once it gets into the afterlife, it's justifiably difficult to suspend disbelief. As a hard sell, though, it's damned effective, emphasis on the damned: if we can't give people adequate reason to listen to us in this world, invent a next world and use that. That leap of imagination can be crass, as in the Catholic

Church's selling of indulgences, or deadly, as in the many virgins (or raisins, as some Quranic scholars have interpreted the text) promised to martyrs in the next world.

This obsession with what comes next is not only depressing but also illogical. If God created all the wonderful things in the world, the mountains and waterfalls and rainbows and mangoes and back rubs and kittens, why are we encouraged to look forward to something else? Obviously, it was savvy marketing in the Dark Ages, when mangoes were hard to come by, but nowadays it just seems like a recipe for an unhappy life. Why spend all our time here—the only time we definitely know we have—waiting for something better?

Judaism doesn't get a complete pass on this one, but it is a marked improvement over the dog-free afterlife of Catholicism. Jews are technically waiting for the Messiah, and it is for his messenger Elijah that the extra plate is set at Pesach. But Reform Judaism has watered this down to a Messianic Age, which likely helps reduce the potential nut jobs declaring themselves the Messiah and interrupting family dinners. When I asked our rabbi about this, he first said that he'd missed that day at rabbinical school. (This was his standard deadpan reply, and I must admit it's a good one.) He then explained that religion is basically a game of 52 pickup: every faith deals the same cards, but the order varies. Jews can believe in heaven and hell, but that card is at the bottom of the pack and rarely gets played.

Once you're in the ground, you're in the ground. You're mourned, and then people move on. If something more exciting happens, well, we'll find that out in due time. That was my understanding of what Jews believed happened after death. I was pleased to see several thousand years of beautiful tradition dovetailing with my personal views.

In fact, I was so comfortable with the whole concept that I didn't mind when Sarah decided not to go on our trip to the funeral home. Her excuse was a good one: her film had been accepted at the Worldwide Short Film Festival and the opening party was that night.

"Are you sure you don't mind going alone? You could probably skip this one, too. There's a good chance this party will have mini-burgers," Sarah said as I was rushing out the door to work.

"I can do both. I'll get the speeches at the funeral home and the food at the party. And better to save my absence for a really boring class."

"Uh, dude, you're going to a funeral home. A funeral home in the middle of nowhere, where you will be reliant on the kindness of crazy classmates to make a getaway."

"You're saying it like someone's actually dead. It'll be much easier to stay awake when we're walking around."

"Your devotion to Jewish study is admirable."

"I promise not to get sleepy and curl up inside a casket."

"Please extricate yourself as soon as possible so you can come to the party."

I kissed her goodbye and left the house, assuring myself that everything would be fine. Sure, the class was often irritating, and it helped to have her there to share the suffering, but one night flying solo was perfectly manageable. Look at Dave, the only single person in the class: he did this by himself every week. Of course, he also told long, irrelevant anecdotes about his lonely bachelor's life for no apparent reason, so maybe he wasn't the best example.

When I arrived at the funeral home after a half-hour taxi ride through the land of strip malls and highways, I felt as though I'd arrived in the distant past. The place had been built in the early 1970s, and I recognized the neo-brutalist concrete architecture from the more depressing buildings on the McGill campus. Inside, the decor appeared unchanged since those days.

I found a few other classmates milling about, but attendance was sparse. No one else had short films in competition, so they must have had other excuses. We chatted awkwardly until a short, curly-haired man came out to greet us.

"So, this is the Jewish Information Class!" he proclaimed, rubbing his hands together. "So glad to see you all. Usually my father gets to meet this class, but this time I was lucky enough to have the honour!"

After a brief tour of the lobby's Judaica, all of which appeared vaguely kitschy but was, we were assured, infused with great meaning—"If people come early and have some time to spend here, we hope it offers comfort"—we were led into the main chapel for the funeral director's lecture on death.

It was a speech he had given many times before, and he had magnetized visual aids to prove it.

The key word was "respect," and he attempted to turn it into one of those call-and-response tricks that only the best orators can ever pull off. Everything about the Jewish burial process came back to respect, and we were supposed to belt that word out like Aretha Franklin.

Why is someone appointed to watch over the body from time of death to time of burial? Respect! Why do we bury the body so soon after death? Respect! Why aren't autopsies allowed? Respect!

It was a bit tiresome, and the lecture only went downhill from there. I had no problem with a bit of Jewish triumphalism—everyone likes a strong sales pitch for the product they're about to buy—but this guy went over the top.

"The way the secular world looks at death is cause and effect," he explained. "Look at the headlines in the newspaper: 'More soldiers killed in Iraq'; 'Freak cyclone kills thousands'; 'Man hit by car.' What does that suggest?"

I wanted to whisper to Sarah that he was reading the wrong section of the newspaper, as all the headlines in my section are much punchier than those. But I had no one to share that comment with.

"What it suggests is, if you stay out of Iraq, you won't die! If you avoid the cyclone, you won't die! If you look both ways before you cross the road, you won't die! The Jewish perspective is a different one, but you can still find it in the paper. Does anyone know where?"

I wanted to suggest the Jumble puzzle or maybe *Marmaduke,* but again I had no one to suggest it to.

The funeral director readied a big magnet and slapped it on the white board with gusto.

"Births, Deaths and Memorials!" he proclaimed. "For Jews, they are all part of the same continuum! Everything that is born must die, and it is right and proper that we have a memorial. Judaism has been grieving for thousands of years, just as modern psychology recommends!"

All of this echoed my previous conclusions, but somehow, coming out of this guy's mouth, none of it was reassuring. He then proceeded to take us through the stages of mourning for both the body and the survivors. He explained how, first and foremost, we needed a body to bury, but in the case of homicide bombings in Israel it was acceptable to bury a body part if that's all that could be found. Now, I certainly don't have any sympathy for suicide bombers, but I do like words to have some meaning. Any "successful" bomber is a homicide bomber, after all—we don't call them killer assassins. Obviously, the intent is to devalue the life of the bomber, but to do so at the expense of logic is just silly. Again, all of this would have been whispered to Sarah but for her being half a city away, enjoying mini-burgers. I tuned out for the rest of the lecture, having decided this guy was too ridiculous to merit my full attention. After what seemed like several hours, he wrapped it up and explained that the tour portion of the evening was about to begin.

First, we went downstairs to see the various rooms in which mourners were consoled. There were many of them, and our guide noted that all of them were designed to look exactly alike so the bereaved wouldn't notice if they were in a different room than the last time they buried a relative. I wasn't sure how this was reassuring, but didn't comment.

Next, we moved into the casket showroom, and here I wish to this day that I did comment. As we'd learned in class, Jewish tradition holds that there is only a simple burial shroud. Provincial law requires a casket, but the plainest of pine boxes is supposed to be good enough.

The ancient rabbis wouldn't have been too happy with the luxurious coffins on display here. Do you like this pine one? We can upsell you to one with slightly nicer handles for just a few hundred more! And why not impress the neighbours with the Rolls Royce of caskets, which will set you back only a bit less than an actual Rolls Royce. Where you're going, you don't need the money, right?

I was reminded again of my fictional mentor, Walter Sobchak in *The Big Lebowski,* who notes the price of the urn required to transfer his good friend Donny's ashes to their final resting place. When he asks incredulously why it costs $180, he's told by the soft-spoken mortician that they range up to three thousand. Astounded at the cost, he loses it: "Just because we're bereaved, doesn't mean we're saps!" On this issue, he has Jewish law on his side.

Again, I tuned out for the remainder of the tour, only registering the frown on the funeral director's face when someone dared ask if he watched *Six Feet Under.* ("No" was his full reply.) As we returned to the lobby, I realized that I was going to need a lift to the subway. The couples managed to pair up pretty quickly, but I was offered a ride by Beauty and the Geek, the jDate couple whose actual names were Shlomo and Maria. I accepted and climbed in the back of their big black Lincoln, wondering why the windows were tinted.

"So, thanks for the lift."

"No problem," said Shlomo, who could in fact see over the gigantic steering wheel. "What did you think of the tour?"

"It was . . . educational," I said. "I know I don't want to be buried there."

Silence followed.

"How is your business going? You distribute films, right?"

I remembered Sarah saying something along those lines and figured if I steered the conversation to his work, there'd be more than enough subject matter to get me to the subway station.

"No, I don't do anything like that. I run my own business out of the home."

He didn't elaborate as to the nature of that business, and I wasn't sure if I was supposed to ask.

"How's business?" seemed a safe enough query.

"Very well. We're doing very, very well."

Another silence followed, though thankfully this one ended with a sighting of the subway.

"Well, thanks so much for the ride," I said, a few blocks too early. "I guess we'll see you next week! Sarah will be back by then. And it's our last class of the spring. Should be a good one!"

I jumped out of the car and entered the northernmost outpost of the transit system, only then realizing I was famished and cranky because of it. Low blood sugar probably didn't help during my funeral-home tour, and the bag of barbecue potato chips I obliterated on the subway ride downtown was an inadequate stopgap solution.

When I emerged from the underground after eleven long stops, I got a call from Sarah telling me the party was still in full swing and that I should head down. I'd forgotten, and the thought of a wasted token triggered more than $2.50 worth of exasperation. Grumbling, I got back on the subway and travelled another six stops and eight blocks to get to the venue.

"What took you so long?" Sarah asked in an incredulous smiley way that, at that moment, was profoundly annoying.

"What do you think? The Jewish way of death! Do you have any idea how far away that place is? How do you think I got here?"

"I just didn't understand why it took so long, that's all. Look, Chewbacca's here."

Sarah and the wookiee from *Star Wars* had a long history together, dating back to the time in junior high when she had overheard kids talking about Chewbacca and asked, "Who is that? Does he go to this school?" She was called Chewbacca for the rest of her junior high days—though I can attest that the physical resemblance is nonexistent—and has since made not having seen any of the *Star Wars* movies a point of personal pride.

The movie *Wookiee at Work,* a short film that imagines what would happen if Chewie were an office temp, was one of the festival highlights. The star came over and put his arm around me. I scowled and backed away. He moved toward Rachel, my fiancée's date for the evening, and I pulled Sarah aside.

"I don't think you understand how horrible tonight was," I hissed at Sarah.

"You were the one who wanted to go."

"Well, that was a mistake."

"I didn't ask you to do it. You wanted to do this, just like you want to be Jewish."

"I do, but I don't want to be Jewish by myself. I spent the night looking at coffins while you were drinking free cocktails and making fun of some lecherous old man who claims to be Norman Jewison's lawyer."

"For the record, he grabbed Rachel's bum, so he *deserved* our mockery."

"For the record, I only want to be Jewish with you. Can we just be Jewish together already?"

"Of course," Sarah smiled. "We can be Jewish together for the rest of our lives."

"And in the world to come?"

"And in the world to come."

I kissed Sarah, and at that moment a slightly tipsy Rachel came over and hugged us both. "You guys, I just want us all to be together," she said. "And now that I've had my picture taken with Chewie, I have a brand new profile picture for jDate!"

The Holocaust and Holokitsch

Every facet of modern Judaism, from Israel to the way prayer is said, is shaded by the Holocaust. To even begin to think about conversion, you have to understand it, yet the enormity of the event makes such understanding nearly impossible. The traditional starting point is the number six million, a figure so massive it numbs the mind. I really only began to grapple with what the Holocaust meant when I met Helena Lazarovic, Sarah's paternal grandmother.

She was five feet tall, wore big glasses and had survived Auschwitz. She lived in a concrete high-rise in Côte Saint-Luc, a very Jewish suburb of Montreal. The Castel Royale, as her assisted-living complex was grandiosely titled, offered its residents such weekly enticements as Current Events with Hershey Dwoskin, Jewish Wheel of Fortune, The Oprah Winfrey Club and shuttle buses to the nearby Cavendish Mall (a.k.a. the Cavenyiddish Mall).

Sarah and Becky regularly made pilgrimages from the multicultural downtown to this monocultural suburb. Their father was an only child and lived more than 1,500 miles away, so these visits were very important. Soon after Sarah and I started dating, I was invited out to the Castel Royale.

When you arrived at the building, you were immediately greeted by a line of wheelchair-bound residents out for some fresh air. (Those with oxygen tanks were presumably just out for the view.) The lobby was similarly packed with chairs, walkers and canes. It could take a while to navigate the ten feet to the elevator. Once inside, we examined the bulletin-board listing of weekly events and regretted that we'd missed Mr. Dwoskin's current events session.

Walking into Helena's apartment, you first had to adjust your eyes to the dimness and then adjust your lungs to the lingering cigarette smoke. In the concentration camps, Sarah had told me on the drive over, her grandmother had traded food for cigarettes. I didn't know how to process that information, so I simply said "Huh." I later figured out she'd earned the right to smoke as long as she wanted, lung cancer be damned.

"Hi, Helena, my name's Ben." I said this loudly, perhaps too loudly, and leaned in for a smoky kiss.

"Hello. So you are Sarah's boyfriend?" She spoke curtly with a thick Czech accent.

"I am."

"And you are staying for dinner?" I didn't think we were,

as it was three in the afternoon, but I remembered we were now on Old Person Time and quickly reoriented myself.

The apartment, furnished entirely in hues of brown, felt like the old country, albeit inside a high rise. While all five feet of Helena Lazarovic busied herself in the kitchen, Sarah brought over photo albums to show me.

We'd been dating for only a few months, so this was more of a smile-and-nod exercise on my part. "Here's my dad with this person you don't know, that person you don't know and this whole other side of the family you don't know." If I'd taken notes, it would have been helpful at later occasions.

Well before 4 p.m., dinner was ready, and if I'd had that notepad out, I would have jotted down the menu. As it was, I remember pushing the food around my plate and politely accepting seconds of something bland. Sarah had told me what an amazing cook Helena had been, rhyming off the Czech specialties she'd make: the best schnitzel, spaetzle, roulades, chocolate sponge cakes, chocolate danishes, jam dumplings and a little-known Eastern European dessert called the chocolate chip cookie.

She wasn't able to cook like that anymore, or so the family learned when cigarette ashes started showing up in their meals. Indeed, by the time I met Helena, she was in slow decline. She made a point of repeating that, despite her hard life, she didn't complain. At the same time, she would lament how old she had become.

This, I understood. My grandmother Laurette had familiarized me with this sort of contradiction. "Oh, this hip," she'd say. "I'm too old! I wish God would just take me now!"

"No, Nan, don't say that!" I'd cry when I was younger, falling into her carefully set trap.

"If God did that, who would give me frozen KitKats?" I say now, ably defusing the pity bomb.

Of course, even if the ravages of age are equally unkind to everyone, Helena's experiences meant it was impossible to make any sort of comparison with anyone I knew. This woman had survived history's most infamous death camp. I knew that early on, but it grew in my mind to the point that I didn't really know what to say to her. If she was dour, well, she certainly had the right to be. Don't complain? Why not?

We'd learned about the Holocaust in school, but just as one part of the Second World War and certainly not in a way that challenged adolescent minds to grapple with its enormity. It was an unthinkable event, so I didn't think about it. The Nazis were bad; that's why Indiana Jones fought them, right? This was simply the proof. My additional knowledge was accidental: while looking for some distraction from chemistry homework in high school, I found Primo Levi's *The Periodic Table.* Each chapter is named for an element, and the whole it creates is a devastating Holocaust memoir.

I knew Levi committed suicide shortly after the book was translated into English, throwing himself down a flight of stairs in 1987, and that fact stuck with me. If even the most eloquent writer, one whose memoir was called a "work of healing" by *The New York Times,* decided forty years later that he couldn't continue, how could anyone? How could this serious little woman, who had lost much of her family and nearly been destroyed herself, live on to make jam dumplings? This, I'd realized from the Woody Allen movies I'd seen, was just the beginning of the series of unanswerable questions the Holocaust raises. Every time I saw Sarah's grandmother, I'd think of more. I wasn't about to interrupt dinner with queries that would reveal just how little I knew.

"Your boyfriend's not Jewish?" Helena said to Sarah shortly after that first visit. "You know I have bad experience with gentiles." That seemed like both an overreaction and an understatement. I couldn't blame her, but it didn't exactly make it easy to get to know her.

When a woman is tired of ChapStick, she is tired of life. That's how Sarah began her eulogy for Helena two years later. As the cancer weakened her, Helena didn't have the energy to keep applying lip balm. It was at that funeral, on a cold, grey Montreal day, that I began to get a better sense of who she was. After the war, she had walked from Poland to Czechoslovakia, where she met her husband; emigrated to Israel, where life was difficult and her son was born; and eventually ended up in Canada, where her brother was. Because Sarah had two sisters and her father was an only child, I was asked to be a pallbearer. I realized it was more about my Y chromosome than my importance to the family, but still, I was moved. As per the tradition I would later study, the procession to the graveyard culminated in each of the mourners shovelling a bit of earth on the coffin while Hebrew prayers were read.

It was then that the possibility of becoming a Jew first occurred to me. This woman had survived Hitler but not cigarettes, and now she was gone. If knowing her inspired me to convert, it would be one more small posthumous victory for the Jews. I enjoyed a thought exercise that made me central to world history and realized that it was more than a touch grandiose. Still, we *were* standing in a windswept graveyard, and this was the death of a survivor. I knew this was an important moment, though it was so unlike any other in my life until then that I had no idea what to do with it.

In the years that followed, the only times I really thought about the Holocaust came at the cinema and in conversations afterward. The existence of a Holocaust genre in Hollywood is inherently problematic, but it was useful in the way it helped me figure out Helena.

I hadn't seen *Schindler's List* back in 1994, and I remember thinking at the time, "Why would I want to go to a movie that's going to be so sad?" I knew enough about it to get the *Seinfeld* joke in which Jerry is castigated for making out during the film ("We just kinda started up a little during the coming attractions and the next thing we knew, the war was over"). That seemed sufficient.

I had grown out of that excuse by the time Sarah and I went to see *The Pianist*. The film tells the true story of Wladyslaw Szpilman, a Jewish musician who just barely made it out of the Warsaw ghetto, and as Roman Polanski's first direct confrontation of the Holocaust—the director survived the Krakow ghetto—it was universally praised. When I walked out, though, I couldn't agree. I had put my arm around Sarah as she cried in the theatre, but for me, something didn't connect.

"Did you like it?" I asked her.

"It was very good. Adrien Brody was really astonishing. Just in his eyes you could see everything. What did you think?"

"Well . . . he was very good in it."

"And?"

"I don't know, it just didn't do it for me."

"What do you mean?"

"Well, it kind of dragged on—you know, his wanderings."

"Dragged on? Of course it dragged on! It was the war! It went on for years!"

"I know, but you knew what was going to happen. He goes from one burned-out building to the next, and it gets worse and worse."

"Well, that's what happened. It's a true story."

"I just feel like, well, like I've seen it before."

"You've never seen his story."

"No, but I've seen stories like it. I've seen *Life Is Beautiful,* and I've read *Maus.* It's just that, as a narrative arc, it's horrific and disgusting and deplorable, but by now it's familiar. I just don't know that it needs to be done again unless it can be done differently."

"Are you saying that we've had enough Holocaust movies?"

"Well, no, but . . . maybe."

"Don't you think every survivor should tell their story?"

"Of course, but they don't all have to be big-screen feature films, do they?"

It wasn't an argument, really, but I felt I had somehow ended up arguing a morally questionable position. How could I say that? How did I go from not enjoying a film to sounding like I was bored of the Holocaust? I didn't think that was how I felt, but as I played back my logic, Sarah's point seemed to hold up. What was wrong with me?

I didn't figure it out then and there, and Sarah and I didn't speak of it again—not on purpose, I don't think. I was reminded of it years later while watching an episode of *Extras,* Ricky Gervais' BBC series featuring self-skewering appearances by film stars. In a now-famous cameo, Kate Winslet plays a crass version of herself making a film about nuns who saved Jews during the Holocaust. Though she felt there had been enough movies about the subject—"We get it, it was grim!"—she had to do one to win an Oscar. (The fact that she finally won for playing an SS guard in *The Reader* provided an uncomfortable coda to the episode.)

The show brought back the wave of discomfort that had followed our post-*Pianist* conversation. This time, I resolved to figure out why. My first thought, something I'd never even heard of back when I saw *The Pianist,* was compassion fatigue. I had been affected by earlier Holocaust movies like *Life Is Beautiful*— a bit embarrassing, given Roberto Benigni's subsequent fall from grace and how terribly the film has aged—and perhaps that had something to do with my lack of response to *The Pianist.* The second conclusion I came to was that maybe I was right: maybe the movie just wasn't that great. In thinking that my reaction was the issue, I was essentially treating Polanski's film as a window on history. Sometimes, you just don't like a movie.

I thought back to a lecture I had covered for the *Daily* in 1999, when Art Spiegelman had visited our university and introduced me to the word "Holokitsch." I dug out the bound volume of the newspaper and read the article again.

Spiegelman began his lecture by explaining that Miramax Films had approached him to design a poster for Benigni's film.

They screened it for him and said that *Maus,* his Pulitzer Prize–winning graphic novel, had inspired it. He refused to do the poster. "I was really perturbed by this movie," he said. "I wasn't upset by the fact it was a comedy. I mean, that's not in and of itself an impossible thing, though it'd have to be so funny you scream in pain." What made him uneasy was that his work had "paved the way for turning mass extermination into mass entertainment."

"*Maus* takes a certain risk, using metaphor to get at something very hard to get at otherwise. Benigni uses the Holocaust itself as a metaphor for a big bummer. Even if you're involved in a really big bummer, as long as you have a song in your heart, everything will be okay."

Now, that came closer to how I felt about *The Pianist.* If I watched both films again—and that doesn't sound like a very fun evening—I hope I'd agree with both Spiegelman and Sarah.

By the time I saw *The Counterfeiters,* the Austrian movie that won the Oscar for best foreign film in 2008, I was well advanced in my Jewish education. I'd like to think that wasn't the only reason I found it to be much better than any of the other Holocaust films I had seen. It told a story riven with moral complexity, one I had never seen or considered before. How would anyone react if forced to forge foreign bills to destabilize the Nazi's enemies? You could refuse and be sent to the concentration camps, or do it and know that you were saving at least your own life. The German soldier charged with overseeing the operation tries to be kind to the men, or at least as kind as he can manage to be to prisoners officially designated as an inferior race. Sarah and I talked about the movie for days afterward.

Of course, maybe the problem is much simpler than the

quantity or quality of the films. Maybe it's encapsulated in that Theodor Adorno line that "writing poetry after Auschwitz is barbaric." Art can be soul-stirring and thought-provoking, but given how much of it there is, it's statistically more likely to be dull and derivative. Combine that with a horrific and nearly incomprehensible event on an unfathomable scale, and the result is all but guaranteed to underwhelm.

So, what is to be done to preserve the memory of the events without mining them for melodrama? This was the question that brought me back to Helena's funeral and one that came up during our class on the Shoah—a Hebrew word meaning a great catastrophe and used synonymously with the Holocaust—and our visit to Yad Vashem, the national Holocaust museum in Israel. More specifically, how could I begin to understand the Holocaust as Sarah understood it? This was my most immediate concern.

The answer, I realized from our lectures in class and our visits to Holocaust museums in both Toronto and Jerusalem, was simple: simply bear witness. Eschew the sweeping piano scores for the detailed stories of survivors. Follow one true story and you can then have some hope of understanding what happened.

That was the intention of the University of Southern California's Shoah Foundation Institute, the project Stephen Spielberg established after making *Schindler's List*. They interviewed Helena Lazarovic in 1997. I watched the DVD a decade later. I ended up doing so alone, on the computer. Sarah had expressed an interest in watching it as well—she remembered finding the interviewer's questions unnecessarily mean to her bubby at the time and wanted to see if that was in fact the case. As it happened, she was away when I decided to confront the subject.

In the interview, Helena faces the camera, wearing a red blouse with white polka dots. She sits at a table in a generically furnished room and is fitted with a clip-on microphone. Her interviewer is a middle-aged woman wearing hoop earrings and lots of mascara. My first impressions of her prove inaccurate, as her interviewing ability is devastatingly effective.

The interview begins with simple establishing questions.

> Q: *When were you born?*
> A: November the 17, 1919.
> Q: *And where were you born? The city and country.*
> A: Volové, Czechoslovakia.
> Q: *Do you remember any specific interaction you had with [your father], something that you did with him that stands out in your mind?*
> A: Yes. Shabbat morning we used to read the Bible together, and I used to translate it. He was very proud.

The interviewer then teases out details of exactly what Helena did when things were getting worse. The matter-of-fact explanation of her bravery is quite effective.

> Q: *When did you realize you had to leave your home?*
> A: To leave the home?
> Q: *Yes, when did you realize you had to leave, when you left your home in Czechoslovakia.*
> A: Nineteen forty-one, we were selected to take us over to the Polish side. We were close by, twenty-five, thirty kilometre from the Polish border. So they

selected us too. But we were very well known and we had help from gentile people, and they let us go home. But a lot of people, they put over the Polish border. And then they start, little by little, to come back through the woods. We had the people working in the woods, and they used to come at night and tell us so many people are there and they need help. So I had two girlfriends, gentile Hungarians, and they had a boyfriend who had a car, so they used to go at night and pick them up and bring them in. Across the street we had a little synagogue. We used to take them there and wash them up and put clean clothes on them and hide them.

Q: *So you were hiding the Polish—*

A: That was our people, from our country. From Volové and surrounding areas. And then one day I went on the bicycle and I stopped on a bridge facing the Jewish cemetery. I was singing a song. Suddenly I see a man, movement of somebody coming out from the cemetery. I looked at him, and he was carrying a little attaché case. So I waved to him, and he came under the bridge, and I told him, "Don't be afraid, I am *amhew.*" He says, "Oh, I am glad to see you."

Q: *What does that mean?*

A: *Amhew?* Jewish, and Hebrew. So I says to him, "You wait here, hide under the bridge, I will be back when it will be dark." So we have connections with the police. They were paid up, the high police officers. I went with the bicycle. We had a signal: I turned around three times in front of the police station, that I need him. So he came down in the lobby, and I said, "I have somebody, I want to take him into the big synagogue." He says, "Okay, I will watch you." So I took him there, and we arranged false papers. The next day by truck, we sent him away. And we did that many times.

Q: *What made you make that choice to help these people?*

A: My brother was a very good Jew. He was recognized as somebody in our place because he helped a lot. If somebody was in trouble in the law, or something, he was everywhere and he helped for everyone. We were brought up that way, to help people.

The family's police connections tipped them off that Helena was to be arrested, so she went into hiding in nearby towns for several weeks. When the threat had passed, she returned to her village.

Q: *So you went back home. What happened then?*

A: I stayed home. It was already beginning of '42. And then in '43 we had the curfew, and we had to wear the yellow stars and we weren't allowed to go out, we weren't allowed to listen to the radio or read newspapers, nothing. But we had a Hungarian engineer who worked for us. He used to come late at night and bring us the newspaper and tell us what he heard on the radio. And that's how we went along till '43.

The interviewer may have seemed harsh to an eighteen-year-old Sarah because she didn't shy away from the most uncomfortable parts of Helena's life. Of course, to do her job properly, she needed to extract these details as clearly as possible. On the cattle car from the ghetto to the concentration camp:

> Q: *What do you recall of any conversation on that cattle car, with your family or with anybody else?*
>
> A: We had a friend of my family there with his daughter. His daughter was my best girlfriend. And he said, "Don't worry, we are going to a camp to work." And I know where we are. We are going to Hungary, to the main land, on farms to work. But then the second day, when the Germans opened the door to the train, and I said before, they asked for money and jewellery, we looked out and we saw a station with a Polish name. And so we started to talk about it. "We're not going to Hungary, we are in Poland, in Polish territory." Nobody liked that. They wouldn't answer us, the Germans, when we asked where we were going. They just ignored us. So, until we arrived in Auschwitz, we didn't know where we were going.

Helena was separated from her parents there and would never see them again. Anyone in the family asking these questions would likely have had to stop there. The interviewer pushes on, and Helena follows. Shortly after, she says:

My doctor, with whom I worked in the ghetto, she
says, "Come on, I have poison. It doesn't look good.
Let's do it now before it's too late." I said, "No, I
don't want." She says, "Come on"—she begged me.
I discouraged her. I took the needles, I broke them
and threw them away. She's alive. She survived too,
but not her husband and not her two children.

After six weeks in Auschwitz, Helena and her two sisters
were moved to a munitions camp, where they built bombs. She
reveals another small detail:

We were lucky. My sister Lea, she didn't want the
tattoo. So, when we were in line for the tattoo, we
always managed to go in the last row. So we escaped
that.

By that point, it was January of 1945 and the war was starting to turn. With little warning, the thirty women working in the
factory, including Helena and her two sisters, were evacuated by
the two Nazi soldiers, a man and a woman, who were running
the camp. They fled on foot for days, ostensibly heading for Germany. On the third day, they saw a building in the distance with
smoke coming from the chimney. It galvanized them.

. . . My sister Lea, she was the leader, she said, "We
have to do something. We have to make hard snowballs and to beat them to death, and then we will be
free."

Q: *Beat the . . . ?*

A: The German woman and the SS man. We have to
injure them or even beat them to death, but we will
be free. So we start, but they were a few yards ahead
of us, and they are still yelling, "Let's go, let's go."
And we had the courage to say, "We are not going.
We don't want to go to Germany. We want to stay
here." We thought they're going to shoot us. I says,
"We are very far from Germany and we will run
into the Russians and they will kill you." We weren't
afraid that they would kill us. But we told them,
"They will shoot you, what you did to us." There
was a ditch there. We carried the two valises for the
SS man and the woman. They took the two valises,
they opened it, they took off their uniforms and
threw them in the ditch, and put on civilian clothes.
They threw the guns and whatever they had in the
ditch. We started to jump, and then we started to
make hard snowballs to throw at them. They walked
away and they turned back a few times, "Come on
with us, you're going to be better off." "You just go
ahead, we are not going." So they left.

Helena and the others made it to the building in the distance, and there they had their first encounter with the Russians.

The head of the regiment was a Jewish captain and
he said, "You are Jewish, right? I'm Jewish too. I
advise you to leave. We are going to stay here, and

the Russian soldiers are very violent. It's not a place
for you."

On their long trek back to their home, they had another
encounter, the significance of which Helena understates.

> Wherever we went, everywhere was Russian soldiers.
> But one house they didn't occupy. It was a couple
> there, Polish people. "Come in, come in, you can
> stay overnight here." But at night they were bang-
> ing on the door. The Russian soldiers, to let them in.
> That they saw girls going in, and they want them.
> The Polish guy was very nice, he says, "They are not
> here, you made a mistake, look in a different house."
> So they left, and we escaped that danger too.

The thirty factory workers walked for six weeks. Helena
and her sisters returned to their village, or what was left of it.
She ended up in Prague, where she found a friend who confirmed that her brother Ludwig had died in Dachau. Other
brothers and sisters did survive.

At the end of the interview, she is asked four final questions:

> Q: *Why did you come forward now to give your testimony?*
> A: I didn't have the energy. Now I took a tranquilizer
>   to be able to talk and not to choke and not to cry.
>   To calm my nerves.

166

Q: *Did you tell your child about your ordeal?*

A: Yes. I told him many years ago.

Q: *What qualities do you feel you possessed that helped you get through what you went through?*

A: A strong will. That I have, and I always had. A strong will.

Q: *What message do you have for your children, and your grandchildren, and all the other children that will come along, and for the world? What message do you have?*

A: A simple message: Let's hope this will never happen again. Never, what has happened to us, to us survivors.

Watching this interview helped me better understand the Shoah. More importantly, it helped me better understand how Sarah understood the Shoah. I realized that having this sort of family history means you learn about genocide much earlier than any parent would ever want their child to know such a thing was possible. I thought of Debbie's neighbour asking why Sarah always seemed so sad.

Finally, I made the connection that in retrospect seems so obvious. A few days after seeing the video, I sat Sarah down and told her I wanted to explain how I felt.

"If Helena hadn't survived—if she had been too weak in the cattle car, or had accepted the doctor's needle, or hadn't confronted her German guards, or hadn't been protected by that Polish family—your dad wouldn't exist and neither would you," I said quickly, trying to make sure I was arranging my thoughts in complete sentences. "Your grandmother was strong and brave, but she was also lucky. That specific historical circumstance—her one story in six million—led to you and then to us. That means any children we have will be, by blood, survivors like her."

Sarah nodded, her eyes watering a bit, and hugged me. Finally, I felt like I understood.

Rules Followed, Bent and Broken

One of the first things a visiting rabbi told our class was that instead of the easy Ten Commandments we've all heard about, Jews have to follow 613. At first, I thought this was a joke, as 613 seems like one of those numbers you would make up. Six-hundred-and-umpteen would have been funnier.

It's no joke, of course. Jewish thinkers through the ages have combed the Torah for all its strict rules, and they generally arrive at 613. Some have said it's also the number of seeds in a pomegranate, but that's not always the case; others have noted that if you divide the commandments into things you can and can't do, you get 248 positives, which is the number of organs in the human body, and 365 negatives, which is both the number of veins and a forbidden activity for every day of the year. To me, this parsing of numbers suggests there must have been at least 613 Jews with too much time on their hands, but I digress.

By the time we returned to class after our summer break, it felt like we had covered a good chunk of the rules. Learning and discussing what you were supposed to do was easy enough; the hard part, we began to realize, was figuring out how much we actually would do. This didn't appear to be too difficult at the beginning, as many of the 613 rules seemed outdated or inapplicable to us. For instance, number 263: make a parapet for your roof (Deut. 22:8); or number 341: don't practise the art of a *chover chaver*—one who casts spells over snakes and scorpions (Deut. 18:11); or number 461, which directs us to eat the flesh of the Paschal sacrifice on the night of the fifteenth of Nissan (Ex. 12:8); or even number 584, which decrees that the king should not acquire an excessive number of horses (Deut. 17:16).

We could easily agree to an immediate cessation of all serpent-directed magic, but we weren't planning to file a request for a parapet with the municipal committee of adjustment. And certainly, in the event that I am made king, I can commit to keeping only a reasonable number of thoroughbreds.

But as soon as we started this process of elimination, we realized we were going about it the wrong way. From the very beginning, when I got my get-out-of-belief-free card from the rabbi, I planned to continue weighing each of Judaism's tenets with logic and reason. I would follow the ones that made sense and, if not ignore the others, then at least downplay them. But the rabbi's initial statement didn't condone this laissez-faire attitude. He emphasized action over belief, a credo that suddenly became more complicated than it seemed. If you don't believe the rules of the religion are of divine origin, why wouldn't you question them before acting upon them?

We then realized that every Jew—and most certainly every Reform Jew outside of Israel—was in the same position. There were, through general consensus, some rules that no one followed, some that the devout followed, some that the religious followed and some that everyone who identified as a Jew followed.

The biggies became obvious through simple repetition. Every time we went to synagogue—and it was still twice a month—we would be reminded: "The children of Israel must keep the Sabbath, observing the Sabbath in every generation as an everlasting covenant. It is a sign between Me and the children of Israel for ever, for in six days God made the heavens and the earth but on the seventh day he ceased work and he refreshed himself."

This was clearly an important one, and indeed Ruth would remind us that the Sabbath was the holiest Jewish holiday as well as "a day on, not a day off." But how does one recognize such a day? Rest, holiness and joy are the three key attributes in Reform Judaism, but we briefly discussed the elaborate game that more observant strains of the faith adhere to. Here, logic is applied to the Torah and the results end up being quite funny. A book like Rabbi Gershon Appel's *The Complete Code of Jewish Law* is remarkable in this respect; in it, I learned that on Shabbat an observant Jew can

✡ adjust the position of an electric fan BUT not its speed;
✡ insert laces into shoes IF doing so doesn't involve undue effort—that is, if said laces are plastic-tipped or the eyelets are not too small;

✡ ring a doorbell if necessary, BUT ideally do so "in a manner different from the usual, with his foot, his left hand or an elbow and the like";

✡ add colouring to food or drink IF said colouring improves the flavour;

✡ blow up a balloon and seal it with a rubber band BUT not tie it with a knot.

These rules all derive from the Mishnah Tractate Shabbat 7:2, a rabbinical parsing of the Torah in which thirty-nine specific work activities were explicitly banned, grouped into the general categories of making bread, clothes, leather and building a house.

So, what activities are allowed on Shabbat? Temple attendance and Torah study are encouraged, if obvious. Also on the list of recommended activities? Sex! Not just any kind of indiscriminate coupling—this is a major world religion, after all—but a physical expression of love that counts as *oneg*, or joy. Coitus is a mitzvah, or blessing, on all days, but on Shabbat it counts as a double mitzvah.

You are also encouraged to enjoy good food with friends, and to invite new people to your Shabbat table. Have a nap! Read a book—as long as you enjoy it! Lie in the hammock! Go on a walk! These are all officially recommended activities on Shabbat, and all things that Sarah and I could commit to doing.

Then there were the dietary rules. One of the first life lessons Ryan imparted to me when we became roommates back in university was on the importance of food. He's not particularly concerned with where it comes from or how it's made, but he's adamant that it be eaten three times a day.

"When I was younger and interested in philosophy, I would wonder why I felt so wretched all the time," he explained. "Was it existential dread, or the sheer pain of being alive? In part, yes. But mainly it was because I wasn't eating regular meals."

This, he said, was a remnant of his childhood. His mother didn't believe in three meals a day. Now, devotion to that ideal, more than any variant of Christianity, was his religion, and Marie helps him observe it. No decisions or serious conversations are to be carried out when blood sugar is low. Sarah and I are converts to this way of thinking, though we stray every once in a while. They say most couples fight about money, but I think it's more likely food, or lack thereof.

A prime example: on one weekday evening, I met up with my brother after work and we ended up enjoying a pizza and a few bottles of wine in his yard. Sarah was at a screenwriting class and came to join us later, but she hadn't eaten. The pizza was long gone. She wasn't quite "hangry"—that horrible state of being so hungry that every little irritation is magnified tenfold and you feel like you're about to snap—but it was in the offing. My brother had little food to offer, though he did have a pair of burgers in the fridge. Sensing a potential emergency, I fired up the George Foreman grill. Unfortunately, it was revealed to Sarah that the delicious hamburger she was about to be served had been purchased on Saturday and it was now Thursday. I didn't see a major problem there—meat is dry-aged all the time—but that was it for her.

I brought the two burgers out and she clammed up. This wasn't a kosher thing but rather a personal dietary law: Sarah won't touch anything that's even vaguely suspect, whereas I take a perverse pride in consuming food that would otherwise go to waste.

"Come on, have a bite!" I pleaded.

"No, thanks."

"But you're starving, I can tell. Mmm, it's so delicious. Look, it's got fresh mozzarella on it, and I toasted the bun."

"I am not eating a five-day-old hamburger."

"It's not five days old. It's more like four. Besides, it's cooked all the way through," I said, waving it in front of her face.

"*I am not eating that burger,*" she growled.

I then realized what a scene we had caused, and the evening petered out shortly thereafter. The next day, my brother admitted that he felt ill after having a few bites of his burger. I, of course, felt fine. Ryan's theory was once again proven.

On a perfect day in a perfect marriage, Ryan strongly recommends starting the day with a full English breakfast. Eggs and bacon are the mainstays, but some sort of fried potato, beans, toast and tomatoes are strongly encouraged. Once your belly is full, the chances of the day going off course are significantly lessened.

Of course, the bacon part of this meal doesn't quite square with Judaism, a problem that I didn't suffer alone. Long before I purchased my first Jewish prayer book, I bought *Everything Tastes Better with Bacon: 70 Fabulous Recipes for Every Meal of the Day,* a lavishly illustrated cookbook by Sara Perry. To make matters more *traif*—that's the opposite of kosher—I bought the book not for myself but for our friend Jon. He made surprisingly good Try-It-You'll-Like-It Bacon Brittle, and I congratulated myself on a gift that quickly recouped its value.

Of course, I didn't buy Jon the book to shove him off the kosher wagon; like most Jews of my acquaintance, he not only ate bacon, shrimp and bacon-wrapped shrimp, but took a pleasure in doing so that Christians never quite can. It is quite possibly the original guilty pleasure, one that predates the contortion of that term to refer to consumption of any sort of popular culture. In this sense, the guilt is genuine, which makes the pleasure more so.

But why? The Jewish guidelines on what can and cannot be eaten are found in Leviticus, and the gist of them is as follows:

✡ You can eat only meat with a hoof and the ability to chew its cud, the latter proviso eliminating pigs.

✡ You can eat only swimming things with scales and fins, so shrimp are out.

✡ You can eat only domesticated fowl, so no pelicans or owls.

✡ You may not eat anything that swarms or slithers, so reptiles and, with a few exceptions, bugs are out.

✡ No roadkill! Under this proviso, five-day-old hamburger meat might also be frowned upon.

✡ You can't "seethe a kid in its mother's milk." This is the justification for banning milk and meat in combination. Note that this rule is not nearly as direct as the others.

✡ Ritual slaughter must be performed quickly and without cruelty.

All of these rules would be fine if it weren't for the one about pork. Why does it even exist? The very real danger of trichinosis in undercooked pork would have been a logical reason to avoid it altogether in ancient times, but now that we know how to properly cook meat, that concern has, for the most part, been alleviated. As well, the very process of salting and curing pork to make bacon kills anything living in it. There's also the argument that pork is so inherently bad for you that it's better not to eat it, but that's easily refuted by nutritional breakdown—it *is* the other white meat—and that same logic would make an artery-clogging, cow-derived smoked meat sandwich just as unacceptable.

But enough haggling over fine print; it makes more sense to look to the principles underlying the rules. *Traif* originally meant meat procured by causing suffering to the animal. This seems like an ideal definition, one that secular society can get behind. A good Jew shouldn't eat chicken from an inhumane factory farm, but then neither should a good human. The overlap between the definition of kosher eating and the modern slow food movement is heartening, no more so than at our temple's weekly summer Harvest Share.

It's a part of Tuv Ha'Aretz, a North American alliance of community-supported agriculture with a name that means both "good for the earth" and "good from the earth." Every week during the summer, Sarah bikes over to the shul and fills a basket with beets, carrots, spinach, kale, onions and leeks. This satisfies both Jewish tradition and modern trends. After all, the original nomadic Jews didn't have to choose the hundred-mile diet; it chose them.

Is that enough? Our rabbi encouraged us to wrestle with the idea of keeping kosher, something we're more or less committed to doing. My weakness for bacon is well balanced by my respect for this sort of religious guidance: he's not endorsing a flippant parsing of the Bible, but neither is he delivering sermons against the evils of spaghetti alla carbonara.

Indeed, the nice thing about converting the Reform way is that you can do things piecemeal, which in our case might mean peameal. The gentle hope of our educators is that we can come to embrace Kashrut at some point in time. It's not a misplaced hope, and it's good to have a next level of devotion waiting for us. Until then, we decided to practise what we call "kosher-style" Judaism.

Just how Jewish was that? We found out when we were given a checklist in class entitled "To Lead a Full Jewish Life, I Must . . ." It featured twenty-two different things that we were to categorize as Essential, Desirable, Makes No Difference or Essential Not to Do. Under Essential, Sarah and I agreed to list

✡ Accept being a Jew and not hide this fact.
✡ Observe Shabbat in a special way.
✡ Belong to a synagogue.
✡ Live *tzedakah* (a Hebrew word with no exact English equivalent; it's like charity and justice) and be involved in social action projects.

Obviously, these were things we wanted to do or were already doing. By this point, Sarah had returned to her doodling, so I charged forward through the checklist. Under Desirable, I ticked off

✡ Attend holiday services.
✡ Be supportive of Israel.
✡ Attend Shabbat services with some regularity. (I underlined the word "some.")
✡ Have Jewish books and magazines in my home.
✡ Have a mezuzah on my door.
✡ Attend High Holiday services.
✡ Celebrate Passover.
✡ Be well versed in Jewish history.
✡ Be well versed in Jewish beliefs and practices. (For this one, I checked the line between Desirable and Essential.)
✡ Have a *brit milah* ceremony for my son(s).
✡ Have a *brit naron* ceremony for my daughter(s).
✡ Observe Jewish holidays at home.
✡ Marry a Jew.
✡ Have a well-rounded Jewish education.

Under Makes No Difference, I marked only "Wear a tallit," or prayer shawl. I was about to tick off "Believe in God" and "Observe Kashrut," but I couldn't quite bring myself to say that belief in God makes no difference in the pursuit of a full Jewish life. We were more or less told it was okay, but still. I placed check marks on the lines between Desirable and Makes No Difference.

In retrospect, this was a good religious reflex test. If I'd had time to think about these questions and prepare my answers for public consumption, I might have moved more than a few check marks over to the Essential column. These were my gut reactions, though, a good indication of where I stood before I even stood up. It gave me pause and reason to wonder: Would this be enough? If I stood before the *beit din* and said these were my beliefs, would they pass me? And if I actually thought about some of these issues, wouldn't I change my mind anyway?

These were questions I figured I had better answer. Since the number one question answerer in my life at the moment was Jake, I submitted the checklist to him.

"Okay, Ben," he wrote, "speaking as the unofficial *beit din*, I pass you." Relief! But then, he was biased. And there was more. "I will be presumptuous and suggest that supporting Israel should be moved to the Essential column. This needn't mean blind, unwavering support for its every policy or action, but a commitment to its secure existence as the homeland of the Jewish people today." I could get behind that. "Also, I'd probably shift the one about observing Jewish holidays at home to Essential as well, in the context of a family. Not a tough thing to do." All right, he's clearly not thinking of the little ones like the Ninth of Av and the Birthday of the Trees. I could agree with that as well.

Somewhat satisfied—or at least not ashamed—I decided that this typewritten checklist was, for me, more important than the 613 commandments. I pinned it on the wall next to my desk and decided to update it as my opinions changed. Actions mattered, and this was my way to measure my actions. My future father-in-law would pass me, so that was a starting point. I had less than three months left to improve upon that score.

Atonement

Every time my father would phone—once every two weeks, on average—Sarah would make the same joke.

"Mitze's pregnant!" she would whisper as she handed the phone to me.

This was partly my fiancée's idea of a practical joke—my father and his lovely lady friend of a couple of years had no plans (that we knew of) to procreate, though she was almost twenty years his junior—and partly a response to Marie's introduction of the subject into our vocabulary.

Having been married to Ryan for nearly five years, Marie was ready to procreate. Understandably, she wanted their child to have playmates, and thus she began using hints and jokes to advance as many of her peers' biological clocks as possible. Sometimes this would be done in a gentle way—"Don't you think it's time? Come on!" she'd say while tapping her watch with her index finger. More often, there would be diabolical whisper campaigns about any couple that had lasted a year or more—"Do you think that Kate might be pregnant?" Marie would ask Sarah. "We just watched her drink two beers, so I hope not," Sarah would respond. Then one day my father called and the joke was over.

"Oh my God! Congratulations!" Sarah squealed. "That's so exciting!"

I stood beside her, waiting to be handed the phone and trying to determine whether this was perhaps the next stage of the pregnancy joke.

On a literal level it was not, though on a cosmic level it could be construed that way.

"Hi, Ben," my father said once Sarah relinquished the receiver. "Mitze is pregnant."

"So I figured. Congratulations!" I tried to sound excited, though I wasn't sure what the appropriate response was.

"We didn't think it could happen," he continued. I didn't like any of the directions that phrase might lead to. "But we're thrilled that it did, obviously."

Good old WASP discretion saves the day again.

"When's the due date?"

"Well, that's the funny part. It's actually going to be right around your wedding."

"A big week, then."

"Yes, indeed," he said, laughing in his version of a nervous laugh. To the untrained ear, it would sound like a particularly hearty laugh, but I knew better.

"Well, again, congratulations, and thanks for sharing the good news. We should get together soon to celebrate."

"I'd like that. How are things with you?"

I didn't really have much in the way of news that could top this addition to the family, and the conversation ended shortly thereafter.

"So?!" Sarah exclaimed as I returned the phone to its cradle. "You're going to have a new baby brother or sister!"

"Yeah," I said, falling into an armchair. "Half-brother or -sister, technically."

"That's silly! She'll be an Errett, just like you. What does it matter?"

"It matters genetically, but you know, you're right."

"How do you feel?" Sarah asked, sitting on the arm of the chair.

"Well," I began, before realizing I didn't know how I felt. "Surprised," I decided. I sat there for a few moments, trying to figure out how I felt. "Happy?" I wondered aloud, somewhat surprised by my own reaction to the surprise.

"You should be," Sarah agreed.

"You're right," I said, mustering my argument. "Mitze didn't think she could have a baby and now she has one, so that's reason enough for joy. And think about the effect it will have on the family! My dad is starting over; he's back to where he was at my age!"

"Plus, we'll get first dibs on the hand-me-down Bugaboo!" Sarah exclaimed.

"Now he gets to raise a child at a time of his life when he'll actually be able to be there and not working twenty hours a day."

"We can always babysit," Sarah speculated.

"I guess this really changes the course of his retirement if he ever retires," I continued, somewhat dazed. "But in a good way, I think. It changes everything. With us getting married and my dad being a dad again, it's like we hit the reset button. I always said I wanted my relationship with him to change. This is change, all right. Think of it: our kids, if and when they come, will have an aunt or uncle who's only a few years older. My brother and my son could be in the same class. Their children will be playing up one branch on the family tree. Wow. It's mind-boggling . . . in a good way, though."

"I think that's the right outlook," Sarah responded.

"I think so, too. And even if it's not, well . . . it just is. I can't control events, so I might as well interpret them in the best possible way, right?"

"Right!" Sarah said, and kissed me.

This all happened right around the High Holidays, a period in the Jewish calendar that begins with a celebration of the creation of the world. Rosh Hashanah means "head of the year," or new year's day, but there's very little time for excessive drinking and revelry.

Just as God created life, he can take it away. The first ten days of the New Year—the period directly after Rosh Hashanah—are when all of humankind has its fate written in the heavenly books. On Yom Kippur, the day of atonement, the books are sealed. It's God's fiscal year-end, and you have a very short grace period to erase the pencil marks before they're put down in permanent ink. These are the Days of Awe, your chance to make things right.

At the class before Rosh Hashanah, we paused at the first mention of the S-word. Sin is a Christian concept at its core; Jesus died for those of his followers. Jews use different words with different meanings. Actions-over-beliefs means there are no sinful thoughts, only sinful actions. And even these divide into three classes:

Heit. This Hebrew word derives from archery and means to miss the mark. You tried, but you just fell short. Hey, it happens. Don't beat yourself up.

Avon. In this case, you weren't trying to do the right thing. Maybe you cut someone off in traffic because you were in a rush, and frankly you didn't care if it was the right thing to do. You probably should pay more attention.

Pesha. You knew perfectly well that robbing that old lady was wrong, but you went ahead and did it anyway. There are no excuses. In modern Hebrew, this word means "crime."

The Days of Awe involve repentance, prayer and something similar, but not identical, to charity. Like sin, charity is a Christian concept that doesn't quite represent what Jews believe. Charity is a virtue for Christians, and the word itself comes from the Latin for "love." Jews instead use the word *tzedakah,* which comes from the Hebrew for "justice." You are obliged to help the less fortunate, and whether or not you do it in a spirit of love is your business. There's even a scale to determine how ideal your help is, with the best kind being the sort that lets others help themselves.

As a Catholic, I never went to confession, but I understood it was there. Any time you wanted, you could visit a priest and have your sins washed away. As a Jew, you have this option but once a year, and the process is a bit more elaborate. You can't simply tell the priest you slighted someone; you have to make peace with the injured party during the Days of Awe. With this in mind, I arranged to get together with my dad. It was slightly contrived, I felt, but the fact that religion and circumstance had both called for a clean slate was too convenient to ignore.

I arranged a Days of Awe brunch with my father. I wasn't exactly sure what I'd say to him—some more polished version of what I'd said to Sarah, I figured—but I knew it wouldn't be anything like Ruth's declaration to our class. Before the lesson that fell in the middle of the Days of Awe, Ruth cleared her throat and made an announcement: "As you know, this is the time of year when we seek forgiveness from those we have wronged. I know at times I have been harsh with you, and perhaps I haven't been the best teacher I could be. I'd like to acknowledge that and apologize."

I don't think the anti-Ruth contingent of the class, of which I was now a de facto member, immediately knew how to respond. Was this, in a way, part of the lesson plan? If so, was it sincere? Well, it had to be, right? Did she do this every year? Or were we the most combative group she'd come across? I wasn't even sure what I wanted the answer to be. Susan, the outspoken lawyer, spoke up.

"Thank you, Ruth. I think I speak for everyone when I say we accept your apology," the spokeswoman for the anti-Ruthers said. I wondered if this was the part where we were to apologize back. No one did. Ruth smiled awkwardly and continued with the lesson.

That apology felt like a staged version of the real thing, with each side calculating what they ought to say for maximum payback. My father-son brunch wouldn't be like that at all, I decided.

When the day came, I biked over to my father's house and congratulated Mitze. I suggested that my father and I walk to a nearby café for breakfast. At that moment, the exercise felt unnecessarily formal, and I considered that it would work better if everyone knew these were the Days of Awe. That might make it seem like what I was doing was more about me and my religious education. Even so, I opted not to mention it. I ordered a coffee; my father had a glass of juice.

"So again, congratulations," I began. "Sarah and I are genuinely happy for you. Obviously, this was a surprise, but I've thought about it and decided it's the best kind of surprise."

"I'm glad you feel that way. That's what we think, too. Mitze is ecstatic, obviously, and I'm happy too."

"It's definitely good news, a new life in the world coming to parents who will be able to give him or her everything."

"Jasmine said you would be upset," my father said, wincing a bit as he does when he's saying something he doesn't really want to say.

"What?" This was the first I'd heard of my little sister's odd prediction. "Why?"

"I don't know, really. I suppose she thought you'd see it as being upstaged." Suddenly, I began to think that if this was how my siblings expected me to act, I had some real atoning to do—and only a few days left to do it in.

"Not at all!" I said, trying to make sure my genuine surprise didn't sound like amplified fake surprise. I decided complete candour was the way to go.

"I admit I was floored at first—"

"That was my reaction, too."

"—but I've realized it's a happy event in all ways. In a sense, it's an opportunity to have a new relationship, you and me."

"I'd welcome that," my father said, "but I want to make something clear: I've decided I only have time for positive relationships in my life now."

What did *that* mean?

"What does *that* mean?"

"Just that I don't want to spend time worrying that I've offended you, or that you're upset about something I said ten years ago."

Now *I* was the one wincing.

"Funny," I said, speaking slowly and, I hoped, without too much emotion, "because I've decided I only have time in my life for honest relationships. I only want to be around people who say what they're really thinking and don't exaggerate for the sake of exaggeration. I can't guarantee that those relationships are always positive, but I'd rather deal with the truth than slap a smiley face on it."

"That's fine," my father said. "That's fine. Let me rephrase: I don't have time for needless negativity. I don't want to wallow in it, or be around people who do."

"Neither do I," I said, remembering the intent of this meeting. "I apologize for doing that."

That, and the arrival of our breakfasts, helped soften the mood.

"I recognize that I made some mistakes raising you guys, and I hope to correct those this time around," he said.

"That's what I meant about the reset button," I said, then worried I sounded too adversarial. "I mean, the main thing is you weren't around when we were small because you were working so hard to give us everything we had. Now, you have the luxury of setting your hours a bit more."

"That's true, though this does change my work plans. I'll be in my seventies when the kid is in university."

"Wow," I said, having never thought of the timeline from his point of view before. Our confrontation out of the way, we continued discussing the logistics of the pending birth. This, I realized, was a point we had never reached in our few sessions with a therapist. There, I dredged up past grievances and vented while he sat stoically, saying he'd done the best he could. Now it was his turn to be angry, albeit in an indoor-voices/public-place kind of way. We had finally gotten somewhere—where exactly, I didn't know, but a place that was solid enough to move on from. I let him get the bill.

As the Days of Awe wound down, I realized I would once again be without my fiancée at an Important Jewish Event. We had purchased High Holiday tickets a month in advance, but closer to the big day, Sarah realized she had also committed to attending a screening of one of her films at the Ottawa International Animation Festival. With the fall cultural season in full swing, there was no way I could join her. I was on my own for the big day. I did my best to rustle up a Jew to attend with me.

"Would you like to accompany me to temple on Friday?" I wrote to our friend Rachel. "Sarah paid big for her ticket. What, you've got something to do that's more important than being inscribed in the Book of Life?"

But of course, when you're born into a religion, you tend to have commitments on the High Holidays. So, I decided I'd go ahead and do this alone, even if I didn't know exactly what I was doing. I had moved beyond my funeral-home annoyance and was prepared to experience all facets of life as a Jew—preferably, but not necessarily, with Sarah by my side.

It was clear to me that Yom Kippur was serious business, but I wasn't completely sure how serious. The all-day fast was one indicator, though unlike the one time I had fasted before—for the thirty-hour famine as part of a high-school fundraiser for a Christian charity—there was no water allowed. I decided to do it. Debbie wished me a *tsum cal,* or easy fast.

✡ ✡ ✡

The service began the night before with Kol Nidre, a sung prayer whose name means "all vows." Here, the whole congregation declares all the hastily made promises of the past year moot and apologizes to God for having made them in the first place. Anti-Semites have seized upon this as proof that you can't trust a Jew, but it was precisely because of hatred that it exists at all. Kol Nidre came to be during the Spanish Inquisition so that Jews facing either conversion or death could safely choose the former and renounce the vow later. Now, it's taken to mean any vow made hastily or against one's better judgment.

I renounced these vows from a folding chair in a gymnasium, which was the designated overflow room for our temple. As I wasn't actually Jewish, I didn't want to deprive a full-fledged congregant their seat in the temple proper. Plus, I figured this would allow me to sneak out more easily should the need arise.

After that service, you go home and avoid thinking about dinner. Yom Kippur has begun, and there is no eating, drinking, sexual relations or levity of any kind. All your energy is to be spent doing a ton of atoning. As Rabbi Lawrence Kushner is quoted as saying in one of our texts, Yom Kippur is "looking in the mirror and seeing what you're going to look like after you've died." The next morning, I was looking pretty good for a corpse. Before I went to temple, I called Sarah to see how she was holding up. I learned that she had already enjoyed coffee and a buttered bagel.

"You're supposed to fast!" I chided. "I'm fasting!"

"I know, but I just can't function without coffee, or food, for that matter. I just shut down, or worse, I get really cranky. That won't help anyone atone."

"All right, I'm not even Jewish and I don't plan on staying in temple all day, but come on! They say only children and pregnant women are allowed to break fast."

"I've been a Jew my whole life and I've never been able to fast," she said. "I'll make it up in other ways. Besides, if the rabbis knew how useless I am when I'm starving, they would make an exception."

I wasn't about to take this one to a higher power. I rode my bicycle to the Jewish Community Centre, where I saw a large crowd of Jews lining up for the big show. I remembered then the rule about not wearing leather, which explained all the men in dark suits and sneakers. I then began to realize I only knew what I had learned in class. I feared that wouldn't be enough. All these children of Israel took this holiday very seriously. I wasn't even Jewish, and wasn't sure what I was doing here. While these thoughts were racing through my mind, I realized I had better use the facilities before the service began. In my slow panic, I accidentally walked into the women's washroom. The lack of urinals quickly tipped me off, but when I exited I heard muffled laughter. I flushed before I flushed, and briefly considered reminding the gigglers that levity was prohibited.

I returned to the line and made my way into the hall. It was packed with hundreds of folding chairs, but, at the early hour I arrived, not many people. I didn't know how long I expected to stay, but guessed that half a day would be my maximum. Despite the sparse crowd, services began on time.

Among the first and most frequently repeated prayers is Al Chet, which means "I have sinned." If you didn't make amends for all your transgressions over the last ten days, this catch-all prayer takes care of everything. It details at length the many sins you have committed, and it's not optional. In other words, there's no opportunity to delete key passages if you think they don't apply. They *all* apply. Each line begins with "The sin we have committed against You by . . . ," and the whole prayer ends with "For all these sins, O God of mercy, forgive us, pardon us, grant us atonement!"

In between, Jews the world over beg forgiveness for their malicious gossip, sexual immorality, gluttony, arrogance, narrow-mindedness, fraud, falsehood, hating without cause, insolence, irreverence, scoffing, hypocrisy, passing judgment on others, exploiting the weak, giving or taking bribes, giving way to hostile impulses and running to do evil. Of those, I was given the most pause by irreverence, an attribute I always thought of as a good thing. I rationalized that this was closer to its strict definition,

191

more about not revering the King of Kings than thumbing your nose at the high and mighty.

An hour passed and I began to grow restless. Our rabbi was back at the synagogue proper, and I could barely see the learned elder leading this ceremony. With Sarah at my side during regular services, I could bluff my way through the Hebrew prayers, but here I was at a loss, quietly moving my lips and trying not to look conspicuous. At that point, with the room about three-quarters full of observant Jews in tennis shoes, my doubts returned. What am I doing in here? It's a perfectly nice autumn day and I'm sitting in a gym full of strangers pretending to chant an ancient language.

I waited for the first appreciable break in prayers and headed for the door. I figured I wasn't doing myself any favours in God's book by feeling out of place, and besides, Sarah was off eating bagels. I hopped on my bicycle and resumed the activities of a normal Saturday, which that day included dropping a DVD off at a colleague's house in the north of the city. Technically, it was work that shouldn't have been performed on this Shabbat of Shabbats, but I did it anyway. Biking uphill under the hot sun, I was soon reminded of my all-day fast. Food, I could manage without, but water? Despite my moment of weakness in the gym, I vowed to stick with the plan. This was my version of atonement, for this year. When I was a Jew, I would do it properly.

I arrived home a few hours later and tried to busy myself with puttering around the house. Again, this wasn't the point of the day, but I was so parched that sitting still would just make me smack my lips and think of cool mountain streams.

I began to realize that the fasting and the day of minimal physical exertion aren't to be separated. Feeling guilty for trying to have my cake and not eat it too—a day of atonement isn't a morning of atonement followed by errands—I picked up my prayer book and tried to study. I soon fell asleep on the couch, dreaming that my mouth was the bottom of an hourglass, filling up with sand. Sarah's key in the lock woke me up, and I staggered over to the front door. She came in with her bags and a large bottle of Evian.

"Aw, I missed you so much today!" I said groggily. "And not just because you brought water I can't wait to drink."

"I can't believe you made it through the whole day. Just a few more hours! Have you atoned?"

"I'm atoned, rested and ready," I mumbled.

"Ready for the wedding?" she asked.

"What?" In my dehydrated state, I couldn't figure out what Sarah was talking about. I was pretty certain we hadn't moved the date up to mid-September.

"Laura and Craig's! We have to get up there!"

We did, in fact, have a wedding to attend that evening, but my parched brain wasn't entirely to blame for my forgetfulness. After all, the bride and groom had given only a week's notice.

Laura, a very talented senior editor at the paper, had been offered a job at a brand-new English-language newspaper being launched in Abu Dhabi. She jumped at the chance to take part in what might be the last old-fashioned newspaper launch in history, though the fact that Emiratis pay no tax must have been pretty appealing as well. Craig, her fiancé, was a filmmaker and occasional copy editor who was happy to go along for the ride.

Laura and Craig were the youngest and second-youngest members of a local lawn bowling club, and that's where they decided to do the deed on the day of Yom Kippur. Friends brought cupcakes and Champagne, and the weather cooperated. As the sun had dipped below the horizon, I was able to drink a gallon of water and reanimate before the ceremony, which was staged barefoot on the manicured pitch.

Afterward, I loaded a plate up with half a dozen cupcakes, filled a mug with Champagne and found a lawn chair under the veranda where I could begin spiking my blood-sugar levels.

"There you are!" Sarah said, coming up after I'd smeared icing over my face. How are you feeling?"

"Much better, now."

"Wasn't that beautiful? It makes me wish we could do our wedding like this."

"Me too.

We sat in silence, watching our friends begin to dance to barely audible music coming from a pair of cheap iPod speakers.

"You know, it would be a lot of fun to move to Abu Dhabi with them," I said dreamily.

"Really? All that desert and ostentatious wealth? No thanks. Besides, we can't."

"It'd be crazy, sure, but only for a few years. And what do you mean, we can't?"

"I'm Jewish and you're about to be. It's not exactly a hospitable place for Jews."

It was the first time I'd been presented with such a tangible drawback of conversion, and I didn't believe it. "I'm not saying we'll move into a cave next to Osama. We'd just, you know, keep a low profile."

"That's ridiculous. Don't you remember that question-naire?" she snapped.

"What?" I didn't see this change in tone coming so quickly.

"On the questionnaire of things we agreed or didn't agree with, we agreed it was essential to live openly as a Jew and not hide that fact. I can't believe we're even having this conversation," Sarah said. "Especially after you spent the day in syna-gogue! How do you think they'd do Yom Kippur in Abu Dhabi?"

"I don't know, but they probably wouldn't eat bagels." That was a low blow.

"You're not making sense," Sarah said curtly. "And what about your new sibling? We'd never see any of our family over there."

"All right, I'm sorry," I said, realizing that my day of atone-ment had yet to end. "Can we just chalk this conversation up to dehydration?"

Latkes and Champagne

At last, the end was in sight.

We had made it to the class on Hanukkah, the most famous unimportant holiday on the Jewish calendar. After this lesson, we had a week off for the lighting of the first candle, and then the final exam. We just had to make it through one class.

That class was the December Dilemma, and whether we liked it or not, we were going to have a dilemma. The course pack promised "a 'personal issues' session in which the candidates and their partners discuss with their teacher/rabbi the issues and concerns surrounding the celebrations of Christmas with their non-Jewish extended family."

In Sarah's view, there was no dilemma.

"When I was a kid, I was sorta jealous, I guess," she said when I asked her about Christmas. "I never begged my parents for a tree or anything, but the big Santa display at the Boca

Town Center was cool. In high school, me and Reut—my Israeli friend, you met her"—had I?—"we would wear Santa hats and give our friends presents. In retrospect, that seems kind of weird."

"And now?"

"And now I really don't even notice it. I guess because I work at home and don't go to malls or watch a lot of TV. It seemed like it was everywhere when we were kids, but not anymore."

When Bob Geldof co-wrote "Do They Know It's Christmas," he wasn't thinking of Sarah. I essentially felt the same way, though my occupational exposure to several hundred seasonal gift guides, theme stories and Christmas cookie recipes ensured that Christ's birthday would never fly under my radar. But even if we thought we knew what we thought, it was time to delve into the December Dilemma.

The guest speaker for the Hanukkah class was a perky young rabbi from Massachusetts, which meant she called the potato pancakes eaten at that time of year lat-*keys* instead of lat-*kahs*. She assured us that in New England this was the correct pronunciation, though it sounded to me like Mayor Quimby saying chow-*dah* instead of chow-*der*. She also claimed they called challah, the braided egg bread, chal-lee.

Once she set us straight on Jewish New England, she began debunking the significance of Hanukkah, something Jews seem to enjoy doing with the same fervour Christians summon to keep the Christ in Christmas.

"There's really no God involved, and no spirituality," she explained. The celebration was to commemorate a military victory, and the miracle of candle oil lasting eight days was later conflated with this. Furthermore, it wasn't even a good time to exchange presents. That ought to be done at Purim. We learned that dreidels, the Semitic spinners that were handed out in my grade school to balance out all the Christianity, aren't technically kosher.

"In strict Jewish law, gambling is outlawed, so the dreidel is somewhat controversial," she told us. Apparently, though, it earned a special place in Israel's heart during the Spanish Inquisition, when Jews would pretend their nights of illicit Torah study were actually perfectly respectable gambling dens. That's sort of like using a comic book to disguise the fact that you're actually perusing a dry textbook, but such is Jewish history.

Her most interesting conclusion, and one I choose to extrapolate from, was that Hanukkah was an example of how we take what we want to take from Jewish history.

"Some might call this cherry-picking, but it's not that at all," she explained. "It's the Reform way. Nothing about Judaism is neat and tidy. As the prophet Ezra said, 'Those who understand, understand.'" This expression, from the Hebrew *hamayvin yavin,* is quite useful in everyday life, and comes up quite often in Jewish debates. Essentially, it's a way to end them.

That made for an awkward segue into the Dilemma portion of the class, where we were to struggle with the idea of being Jewish in a Christian world. To kick things off, Ruth told a story of visiting a mall with her young son many years before. While she and her husband were able to convince him that the many decorations were there to mark the festival of lights, they weren't agile enough to prevent him from noticing that Santa Claus was heading their way.

"Ho, ho, ho!" the mall Santa bellowed in Ruth's oddly gripping retelling of the story.

"Mommy, mommy!" her child shrieked. "It's a big red clown!"

This was quite funny, but also provided a window into the media-free environment of Ruth's home. Santa came up to the child, said hello and generally didn't notice the parents standing there in shock. He handed the boy a candy cane, chortled again and moved on, presumably to find some children who knew who he was.

"Mommy, mommy . . . is it kosher?" the poor child asked.

To Ruth's surprise, we all laughed.

To ratchet up the tension between Christmas and Hanukkah, we were given handouts that strongly argued against Jews having anything to do with Christian celebrations. One typewritten tract that appeared to date back to the days of mimeography, by Rabbi Roland B. Gittelsohn, argued against everything from tinsel ("meant to recall the heavenly hosts who are supposed to have attended the miraculous birth of the Christian savior") to gift-giving ("meant to 'emulate the amazing unselfishness of Christ'") to mistletoe ("Must we be deprived of this too? I'm afraid we must," he wrote, before noting that it may represent "the crown of thorns Christ wore on the cross, the little red berries symbolizing his blood." It's unclear where the kissing part comes in.).

But he saved his most savage attacks for the Christmas tree, noting that its early Christian use (note the qualifier "early") was based on a legend (i.e., a myth) that the night Jesus was born, all the trees of the forest bloomed and bore fruit despite the snow and ice that covered them. (The heavy snows of Bethlehem being different then, one supposes.) He goes on to argue that the wood in the tree represents the cross of crucifixion, which then makes you wonder why it's not called an Easter tree. Finally, he writes, "Grim irony indeed, that Jews, so many of whose ancestors were persecuted and perished because of their alleged complicity in the crucifixion, should now embrace a symbol of that very event!"

"This is ridiculous!" I whispered to Sarah. "Christian fundamentalists hate the trees and the tinsel and the shopping, and we do, too? Who are they there for, then? Atheists and Muslims?" Sarah shushed me. I didn't really have any particular love of the Christmas tree. The pine scent is a nice one, but it's best experienced when cross-country skiing past live trees in the snowy woods. Plus, who wants to spend January vacuuming up needles? Still, this broadside seemed unnecessary and frankly beneath Judaism. Is Israel really that threatened by the presence of a rotting conifer in the living rooms of its children?

The lawyers in the class, as professional arguers, agreed with this line of thinking and voiced it in class, so I didn't have to. Our mild-mannered guest speaker, while admitting that our reasoning was technically correct, eventually stated that this is simply one of those non-negotiable items. I began to understand why the class organizers were so eager to bring the December Dilemma to our attention. Easter eggs didn't faze the rabbis, nor did the prospects of Mardi Gras parades. But Christmas, with all its glitter and glamour and presents and TV specials, was a soft spot. This was the ground they would never yield. It was beyond logic, but at this point, I was just glad I didn't feel strongly about it.

All this sensitivity later made me wonder about ginger-bread, my favourite seasonal snack and one that all the latkes in the world couldn't replace. I feared some forthcoming hand-out would claim that Catholics used to build churches out of the stuff in the Middle Ages. This admittedly low-level fear was happily dispelled when Rachel presented me with a gingerbread Star of David cookie. I wouldn't run it by Rabbi Roland B. Gittelsohn, but it was good enough for me.

At the end of the class, we were given a study guide with all the questions from the exam. The good news was that we had all the questions right there; the bad news was that there were many, many questions. There were also six pages of Hebrew words, and instead of being in that classical Hebrew font, they were in a script that looked like Inuit text.

"I'm not leaving anything to chance," I told Sarah. "We're going to do this whole test backward and forward until we're Talmudic scholars."

"Sure thing, bean."

We cleared our schedules for that weekend and began our studies. Hearing of our preparations, Debbie sent up several CDs of traditional Jewish prayers to help me get them straight. I thanked her profusely but assured her there was no oral por-tion of the exam. It was Shabbat and studying was work, but it was technically allowed because it was Jewish education. Half an hour in, I was stymied. I didn't know any of this stuff.

I flipped forward to the Hebrew words and reviewed them until my frontal lobe was full of mnemonic devices.

Havdalah, like a halving, or a dividing, as in the ceremony that divides Shabbat from the rest of the week!

Beit Knesset, like the Israeli parliament, means "house of assembly."

Tefillah, as in when you te-fill out your prayer shawl, these are the tassels that dangle below.

Hadlakat nerot—sounds like the emperor Nero, who fiddled while Rome burned. Burning reminds me of candles, and thus this is the Shabbat candle-lighting ceremony.

The more desperate I became to memorize the words, the sillier the devices became. In the same fashion, our irritation with Ruth grew as we read through study questions we'd never remotely covered in class. But I thought back to my university days and realized it wouldn't have mattered anyway: the classroom was where you jotted down notes, asked the occasional question and tried to stay awake. All the actual learning occurred in the days and hours before the exam. If this pedagogical strategy, based solidly on my nearly two decades of education, is ever embraced by the establishment, it will mean either exams at the end of every class or drastically truncated school years with a whole semester being taught in a week. I only ask for credit for my proposal if the latter approach emerges.

Unfortunately, our rabbi was less than impressed by how little I had actually learned in class, as I found out when I asked him for some help on the study questions. I was unable to put the prayers of the Shabbat service in order, which in my defence was a tricky thing to do. Still, I suggested to the rabbi that I both didn't attend services often enough and didn't pay enough attention when I did attend.

Sarah and I ultimately spent a few nights in front of our computers, googling as many terms and names as we had to in order to complete the test. Some of that old multiple-choice trickery was employed in the test, which helped with questions like these.

Concerning the afterlife, Reform Jews believe
a) that there is no life after death
b) that the righteous go to heaven and the wicked go to hell
c) that the body dies but the soul remains immortal
d) a wide variety of opinions rather than a single dogma

Years of experience with standardized tests would have let me get that one right before a single hour of Jewish education. Similarly:

The relationship of a person to God, in Judaism, is one of
a) obedience
b) partnership
c) struggle
d) all of these

But then there were those tricky distractors to catch Christians who weren't paying attention:

Which of the following terms is used by Jews to describe the Hebrew Bible?
a) Tanach
b) Old Testament
c) Pentateuch

d) Five Books of Moses

e) all of the above

It looks like another (e), but then you realize you read option (b) a bit too quickly. It's only the Old Testament if there's a newer one, and as far as Jews are concerned, that's all He wrote. Which was good when it came to memorizing the books of the Bible, because the old mnemonic G.E. Light bulbs Never Die—Genesis, Exodus, Leviticus, Numbers, Deuteronomy—was nice and succinct.

I was puzzling through this at my desk while Sarah worked in the other room. She had to take the exam as well, and her failure would ensure mine. I got to the short-answer question that asked for ten things you'd find in a Jewish home. It sounded like a *Family Feud* showdown, I thought, and I went to see what Sarah had written. I found her working on one of her weekly cartoon assignments, her book closed.

"Hey, I thought we were working on this stuff together," I said, sounding more wounded than I intended.

"We were," Sarah said, "but I've got filming this week and need to get ahead on my regular work."

"Have you answered the questions?"

"No, I figured we'd go over your answers together." I must have still looked wounded. "Aw, come on. You know I sat through all those classes on Hebrew when I can already speak it. Some of those lectures were interesting, but, honestly, I'd heard that all before. And Ruth was a bad teacher no matter if you knew the material already or not. I'm going to help you with this and we're both going to pass, so what does it matter?"

This was when I realized my progression was complete. In the beginning, it seemed to everyone, including us, that I was doing this for Sarah. Then, it became us doing it together. Now, in the final stretch, it seemed pretty obvious that she was searching the web for Hebrew definitions for me.

To thank her, the night before the exam I stopped by the Harbord Bakery and picked up a gingerbread Star of David, the last one they had.

"A present for my study partner," I announced as I presented the seasonal confection.

"Thank you," Sarah said as she opened the package. "It's missing a point, though."

"I got hungry on the walk home. But it's symbolic: Judaism is ours to share."

"But you get first bite?"

"And I leave the rest for you. Plus, I got a lemon poppyseed loaf of no religious significance."

For a final evening, we got down to our Hebrew studies. In total, I had sixteen pages of solid Judaica committed to memory by the time I walked into the final exam, minus a few questions deemed simply unlearnable. I think Sarah knew them all from the first day of class, though I'm sure the studying didn't hurt.

I lined up my pencils on my desk, set my watch in the corner and was off. Everything was as expected, and I worked my way through methodically. Before I was halfway done, Sarah handed in her test, followed by a flurry of other show-offs. I didn't let it faze me. It felt good to work through a test on which I knew every answer, or at least knew which ones I had completely correct and which ones were educated guesses. I wanted to savour this moment, the first test I had written in years, in the hopes that it would somehow erase from my subconscious the nightmare about writing an exam I wasn't prepared for. Sadly, it did not.

When nearly everyone had finished and Ruth called time on the final straggler, she brought up a suggestion that she had mentioned in passing earlier.

"Traditionally, the classes like to all go out together for dinner to celebrate the end of class," she announced. "Does that sound like a good idea?"

"Definitely, Ruth!" a member of her fan club announced.

"I was thinking we could go to King David falafel," she said. "Is that in everyone's budget?"

Just then I noticed a group of the lawyers, led by Susan and Ari, packing up their bags.

"I'm happy to go out for a drink," Susan said, smiling, "but there is no way in hell I am spending another minute with her."

Admittedly, I felt the same way, but for a moment Sarah and I seemed to be standing in the middle of the room, straddling both camps.

"Are you guys going to come?" asked one of the nicer Ruth fans, a woman who clearly had no dislike in her heart for anyone, least of all the teacher.

"Oh, well, what's the restaurant again?" I asked, knowing that I wanted to go with the cool kids even if that meant the un-Jewish talking with an evil tongue.

"King David falafel," my fellow student replied while I

racked my brain for a good excuse to join the unofficial outing.

"That's a fast food–style place, right? After that test and all the cramming, I really need a drink," I said convincingly. "So I think we're going to celebrate somewhere else." Weighing the options, I realized I would rather look like an enthusiastic fan of alcohol than an enemy of the teacher. This may have had something to do with the fact she had yet to grade my test.

My awkward attempt at diplomacy didn't do much to disguise the fact that the fault lines in the class had finally separated. I'd pulled Sarah over to the bad-ass side of the chasm, not that she needed much convincing. We said awkward goodbyes, made all the more awkward by the one elevator everyone had to take down to the parking lot.

Team Bad Ass decided to walk around the corner to the House of Chan, a Chinese steakhouse known as much for its Jewish clientele as its terrifically inauthentic Chinese food.

The eight of us ordered Champagne and filet mignon to celebrate the end of Ruth and the Jewish Information Class. We discussed our mikveh appointments. Susan, the primary Ruth hater, said the teacher had offered to be one of her witnesses.

"There's no way I would let that woman see my secret flower," she said with mock indignation.

We cycled through the list of ridiculous stories and anecdotes Ruth had told us, relishing the ones that incited particularly inane discussions. My contribution was her story during Sukkot, the fall harvest festival that was celebrated with an etrog, a lemon-like citrus fruit. Ruth had heard that, as produce, these were forbidden on international flights and they were being confiscated en masse at the airport.

"It's like the SS all over again," said Dave, the class's loner, which seemed like a joke but sadly wasn't.

And then there were her off-hand comments about the petite female rabbi who had explained the differences between Reform, Orthodox and Conservative Judaism, one of which had escaped my notice until that point.

"Did you enjoy that lecture?" Ruth had asked us afterward, and when someone replied that it was thought-provoking, her immediate follow-up was, "In a good way or a bad way?"

Then we realized the bad thoughts had gone on long enough, and a toast was proposed to Ruth.

"To Ruth," one of the lawyers said, "for leaving us with so much to learn."

"*L'chaim!*" we cheered as we clinked glasses.

Ruth had made a big to-do of telling us how she stayed up all night correcting tests and would call us with the results as soon as she marked the papers, but there was no phone message or email when we arrived home that night, or the next morning, or at all. That, we reasoned, was the price we paid for abandoning the falafel excursion. A few days later I asked our rabbi, who told us that Ruth had given him the good news. We had the knowledge and the classroom hours; now, I was ready to face the council of rabbis.

Fortress of Solitude

"Benjamin?"

The council was ready. The big, bearded, soft-spoken rabbi who summoned me had been a guest lecturer in our class, and I instantly recalled that his synagogue shared a parking lot with the mosque next door. In the winter, they split the cost of snow removal. I pushed this irrelevant thought aside as the rabbi led me down one hallway and then another, and returned to the fundamental question and answer I kept worrying about: God. I was too intent on repeating my action-over-belief mantra to excuse myself from asking if I believed. Now what if they asked that question? Did I? Hidden of Hiddens, Hidden of Hiddens, I repeated in my head. That name for God almost excuses agnosticism. That, I believed in.

I followed the rabbi through a door to find the two other judges sitting at a boardroom table. The brightly lit room with a view of the strip mall across the street was furnished as it would have been in the 1970s, and the Judaica on the wall seemed to date back to that era. I introduced myself to the second judge, a small woman with kind eyes and a big smile. Two for two, I thought. The third judge was a skinny man with a shock of grey hair under a black skullcap. He didn't smile as readily. This was the bad cop, I decided, but he was outnumbered.

"Why don't we begin with you telling us a bit about your spiritual background?" the big guy asked.

"Of course," I replied. "I was born and baptized Roman Catholic. My mother was Catholic, and her family is quite religious, whereas my father's is sort of vaguely Protestant. I went to catechism in grade school, but I first became disenchanted with it very early."

"And why was that?" the lady asked. I realized the story I was about to tell wasn't necessarily one I planned to get into, but she'd asked, so here it was.

"Well, at one of the catechism lessons, they were describing what heaven was like, how it's paradise and it has everything you could ever want. I raised my hand and asked if I could bring Roslyn, my basset hound. The teacher smiled and told me no, heaven was for humans only."

"What did you say?" the woman asked.

"Well, I think I cried. I was in first grade, after all. I think they told me that dogs didn't have souls, which seemed like adding insult to injury. Eventually, either the teacher or my mother said there was a dog heaven, which made me feel better. Still, at that point I knew I didn't want to believe what they were saying."

"But you were still a Catholic?" the leader asked.

"Yes, I still went to church until we moved to Connecticut, and then our family's attendance began to drop off. I studied biology at university, and that really pushed me into the agnostic camp. I was most put off by religious arguments against evolution, which, for some reason, really irritated me. I think it was the idea of arguing against logic with silly examples and wildly implausible theories."

I looked at my inquisitors. The big guy and the woman were smiling, but the skinny man looked nonplussed. I tried not to look at him.

"What brought you to Judaism?" the leader asked.

"First and foremost, my fiancée. The way her family practised, and practises, Judaism feels very right and natural to me. I think specifically of her two grandmothers' funerals, at both of which I was a pallbearer. Both ceremonies were very moving and much more, well, appropriate than any ceremony I had been to before."

Just then, the kindly lady wiped a tear from her eye. I wasn't sure if it was the basset hound or the funerals, but I knew she was on side.

"Who is your favourite figure from Jewish history, and why?" the big guy asked, signalling that we were on to the tests of Jewish knowledge. I was momentarily stumped, but tried not to show it. The first name that popped into my head was Sandy Koufax, but I don't even follow baseball, so I rejected that one right away. Maimonides? At the moment, I couldn't think of a single thing he had written or said.

"Hmm, that's a tricky one," I said in what must have seemed like an obvious stall for time. "Let me think."

I was about to start cycling through the class lectures when I realized that, in my cramming session, I had skimmed over the perfect example.

"Well, I think it would have to be Hillel. I'm thinking specifically of that time someone challenged him to sum up all of Judaism while standing on one foot."

The judges nodded, a good sign.

"And Hillel says, 'No problem. Treat others as you'd like to be treated. That's all there is in the Torah. The rest is commentary.'"

I briefly feared that I had accidentally quoted Jesus instead of Hillel, and in so doing referenced the one Jew I shouldn't reference. But Hillel definitely had said that, right? I realized, wonder of wonders, that there was some overlap.

"But you have to study the commentary," the chief smiled.

"Of course," I replied.

"Why is that so meaningful to you?" he asked.

I didn't say, "Because I read it less than an hour ago." Instead, I said, "I suppose because in this year of learning, there's been a lot of material. Sometimes, it's easy to lose sight of the bigger picture. I like that the bigger picture is so simple, and that Hillel had it at the top of his head."

At that point, the judge I took to be the bad cop asked his question.

"You still haven't told us why you want to be Jewish," he said, unsmiling.

"Oh, ah, okay," I responded, quickly reviewing my checklist. "I want to be Jewish because I want to join the Jewish community. I want to be a full member, and I want to raise our children in it. I want to make a commitment to something much larger than myself. I've learned a great deal about the religion, and I particularly like the emphasis on questioning. As I said before, I had my first problem with religion when I asked a question. If that had happened in Judaism, I would not only have not been so disappointed, but I probably would have been praised for asking a question in the first place. That's my kind of religion. And the Jewish God, the idea of a hidden and unknowable God who is everywhere and in everything, that just makes sense to me."

"Benjamin, thank you very much for answering our questions today," the chief judge said. "If you want to just wait outside, we'll call you in shortly."

I shook all their hands again and returned to the waiting room.

"How'd it go?" Sarah asked.

"Uhhh, good, I think. One guy may not have liked me, but unless he has veto power like the Security Council, I think I've got it."

Soon after, the chief came out and motioned for us both to follow him. I was to go in first while Sarah waited at the door. I walked in and closed the door softly.

"Benjamin, congratulations," he said. "We're happy to accept you as a Jew."

"Thank you!" I said, unsure if it was the right thing to say. Sarah had heard everything and came in right behind me.

"*Mazel tov*!" the kind lady said to both of us, still with moist eyes. Now that was the right thing to say. Sarah saw her crying and started to cry, too. "I wish you every happiness!"

"*Mazel tov,*" said the grey-haired man with a tight smile. Maybe he was outvoted, or maybe he just doesn't get as wrapped up in this stuff as his fellow judges. It didn't matter.

The *beit din* signed a form for our rabbi and we bid them farewell.

"I'm just so happy right now!" Sarah exclaimed as we waited for the elevator. "I didn't anticipate feeling this way at all!"

"You didn't think I'd pass?" I asked in mock umbrage.

"No, I didn't think your passing would matter so much to me," she said. I kissed her.

As we left the building, I noticed Moe Pancer's Delicatessen in a strip mall across the street.

"That didn't use to be there," I said to Sarah. Was this God sending me a message, a bolt of brisket from the blue? No, it was just the historic deli's new location, three blocks south of where it had been before. We had been to the previous location, an old-fashioned lunch counter, on occasion with Jewish friends who claimed it served the closest thing to Montreal smoked meat in the city.

Sadly, we found further proof that it wasn't divine intervention when we went over for lunch. The corned beef was adequate if unremarkable, but the charm had been left in the previous location.

"I'm glad this isn't officially my first meal as a Jew," I said as I chewed my sandwich.

"I'm glad we don't live up here," she replied.

"I'm glad you came along for the ride."

"I wouldn't have missed it for anything. It made me so

happy to see the three of them so happy with you and your words. Of course they would have been happy with you."

We finished up and got back in the car, and Sarah drove me to work. When I arrived, my colleagues congratulated me with a spread of bagels, cream cheese, capers and smoked salmon.

"This is great, you guys," I said, genuinely surprised. "But you know, I'm not actually Jewish yet."

"You passed, though, right?" Maryam said.

"Yeah, but that's only the first step."

"Ah, it's close enough for us. Have a bagel."

If the Hidden of Hiddens wanted me to have two lunches—not that I could ever know Him or what He wanted—it was the least I could do.

The Unkindest Cut

"You're going to have a new baby sister," my father announced.

"*Half*-sister," I almost replied, before thinking better of it and simply exclaiming, "That's terrific. And symmetrical: two boys, two girls."

My siblings' reactions to the news had ended up being the same as mine: shock, amazement and gradual excitement. Now that we knew the gender, the whole thing became that much more imaginable. Jasmine would no longer be the youngest child, thus relieving her of that burden. As an added bonus, she was scheduled to graduate from nursing school in the same week as the baby's arrival, making it as clear a signal of adulthood as she could hope for.

That was also the wedding week, of course, and the prospect of having both my parents in close proximity was stressful in itself. Debbie had preparations under way from Florida while we fine-tuned the guest list. The thought of having all these relatives from different sides of the family sitting in the same room began to worry me. On top of that, there was the dilemma of explaining our new sister to my mother.

Normally, when one parent had major news, my siblings and I would have an unofficial meeting to determine how best to tell the other parent. In our adolescence, my brother and I had seen how events and reactions could spiral out of control if we didn't control the message. As each parent was put on a state of emotional high alert by any news of the other, it was often a case of downplaying the news and trying to reduce its impact.

A baby, however, was difficult to spin. Before we could even try, Jasmine told my mother.

"I just can't believe it. I just can't," my mother repeated to me after she'd heard. "At his age!"

"It's a big deal," I admitted, looking for the appropriate damper, "but it doesn't affect you at all. Don't worry about it. Don't even think about it. Laugh, shake your head and move on. It's immaterial."

"Not to *you* it isn't."

That was true. I was still feeling good about my new sister—I'd resolved to be more accepting, if less accurate. I was particularly relieved that she was a she, a reaction I didn't expect to have but one directly related to my ongoing march toward the tribe of Israel: her gender meant the subject of circumcision needn't be raised.

Now that I'd passed the test, I had reached the *brit milah,* the covenant of circumcision. We were reminded that this was the physical manifestation of the order to be fruitful and multiply. To remind each male of his responsibility to do so, a mark is made in a place he can't possibly miss.

I was fine on this front, I thought, declining the procedure as one would turn down a waiter's offer of dessert. But why, if I could eat bacon (while struggling, of course) and drive on Shabbat without risking the ire of Reform Jews, was this still such a sticking point?

The answer, from our readings: it's just too central to Jewish life, from Abraham—who did it at the ripe old age of ninety-nine, after all—on down.

In *Living a Jewish Life,* Anita Diamant considers the arguments against the procedure before rendering this verdict: "As to the 'why' of *brit milah,* the most compelling reasons are not always the most rational. For many parents the answer to that question is: If we stop doing the *brit milah,* we stop being Jews. Brit milah is a physical connection to the ancient Jewish past and to all subsequent generations to the present day. It is also one of the few ritual practices on which virtually all Jews still agree."

There's even a famous story of the prophet Elijah, who complained to the Lord that the people of Israel had "forsaken your covenant, torn down your altars and put your prophets to death with the sword." The Lord responded: "They shall not observe the covenant of circumcision until you see it done with your own eyes."

Which led to the rule that an empty chair be set out for Elijah at every *brit milah,* so that he may see that the covenant is upheld. In other words, some Jews tried to get out of the covenant, and it didn't fly.

Even with that precedent, some branches of Reform Judaism tried it again, early in the nineteenth century. This was after the emancipation, when European Jews were allowed to become citizens of their countries, and apparently some Jews were so thankful that they decided to return the favour by assimilating as much as they could. They also abandoned Hebrew prayers for German ones, moved Shabbat to Sunday, jettisoned all the dietary laws and declared Germany, not Israel, the new Zion. Obviously, this mindset didn't get very far with most Jews, and the events of the twentieth century obliterated it entirely. The *brit milah,* to adapt a motto, is here, it's severe, get used to it.

And though I technically satisfied the requirements, a technicality wasn't enough. The medical procedure saves you a lot of trouble, but it's not a religious ritual and wins you no points in the eyes of the Lord. You can't luck into having the procedure that makes you a Jewish man; the religious ceremony must be performed. At the beginning of my conversion, I didn't know this and tried to change the subject whenever it arose. Once the process was explained in class, I could no longer deny knowledge of the *hatafat dam brit,* or drop of blood of the covenant. I'd explain this to inquisitive Jews, bracing myself for the double entendre on the word "prick." I wanted the whole thing over with as quickly as possible, so I planned to get it done before the mikveh to avoid the embarrassment of making the procedure the final barrier to my entry into Jewish life.

The dignitary who officiates over such a transaction is called a mohel, which, in case there's any doubt about what's happening, is Hebrew for "one who circumcises." One doesn't have to be a doctor or a rabbi to serve this function, but since many are, why would you settle for anything less than the most fully trained professional? It is one of those occasions when you don't want to be reminded that the tradition is an ancient one; better to think of it as a simple visit to the MD for an elective procedure.

I obtained the name of a respected mohel-slash-doctor from my rabbi and made an appointment early one morning. His office, not surprisingly, was up north in a Jewish area of town. On the commute, I realized I'd gone from apprehension to squeamishness to a fervent desire to get this over with as quickly as possible. I entered the nondescript medical office building, noting several people in the lobby who were almost certainly not there for the same procedure.

There was no wait—it was very early in the morning—and I walked straight into the doctor's office.

"Hello, Mr. Errett," he said. "How are you feeling today?"

"Better once this is over," I said before realizing that this must be the same exchange everyone who comes in here has.

I wish I could describe the mohel, but other than the facts that he was professional, courteous and bespectacled, I couldn't have picked him out of a police lineup a minute after I walked out of his office. He invited me to take a seat in front of his desk as he reviewed my file.

"Now, do you understand the significance of this procedure?"

"Yes."

"And are you aware of what it entails?"

"I believe so."

"Well, then, if all the information on this form is correct, we can get started."

All the information was correct. We could get started. I froze for a moment, then followed his lead to a door I hadn't previously noticed. It led to a small examination room that looked like any other doctor's examination room—bright lights, a sink, a bed covered with a roll of hygienic paper.

"Do I sit on the bed?" I asked, thinking back to past physicals.

"No, that won't be necessary," he said as he prepared the equipment over the sink. I opted not to look closely at what that equipment entailed.

"Okay, we're just about ready to get started. I'm going to ask you to pull down your pants and underwear and hold your penis in your hand."

I followed the instructions.

"Now you might want to look away or close your eyes for just a moment."

For that moment, I had another one of those waves of doubt of the sort I hadn't experienced since feeling like the odd man out on Yom Kippur. I described my surroundings to myself in the starkest terms: here I was, standing with my penis in my hand in a suburban office building while a middle-aged stranger chanted ancient prayers and prepared to jab my genitalia with a needle. This time, unlike my immediate reaction to my outsider's view of the Yom Kippur ceremony, I didn't try to escape. I instead summoned an alternative and no less true version of events: here I was, submitting to a superficial and relatively painless procedure administered by a respected medical doctor to gain official admittance to a religion that would provide me and my family with solace, guidance and instruction for the rest of my life. That wasn't so weird, was it?

In the time it took me to pivot perspectives and ultimately decide not to bolt out of the mohel's office, the deed was done.

"You may notice a spot of blood on your underwear tonight, but that's perfectly normal," the mohel said. "The wound is disinfected. You shouldn't even feel it."

I buttoned up, washed my hands and returned to the doctor's office to sign the official document declaring that this all actually happened. I thanked the doctor and left the office, noticing by the clock in the waiting room that the whole thing had taken less than ten minutes. There it was: the biggest non-negotiable item in all of Judaism done in less time than it takes to get your car washed.

As I walked to the subway, I was again grateful to my parents for making this part relatively easy. I also considered describing the whole process to Sarah in excruciating detail, reminding her throughout that I was doing it all for her. But that wasn't true: I was doing it for myself, and taking the *hatafat dam brit* like a man was all part of that. Of course, there really was no other way to take it.

Strip 'n' Dip

Whenever the ceremonial bath known as the mikveh was mentioned, a distant corner of my brain started singing the adapted theme from *James Brown's Celebrity Hot-Tub Party.*

"Gonna get in the mikveh! Gonna get wet in the mikveh!" was, of course, not exactly how the song went in the *Saturday Night Live* skit featuring Eddie Murphy as the late Godfather of Soul.

Ruth had prepared us for the final step in the conversion by talking about the process in hushed, rapturous tones.

"It's just a very, very special experience," she said. "You probably want to bring a pair of flip-flops or other shower shoes and a bathrobe. Even better, if you're able to do so, you should go out and buy a new bathrobe for the occasion. Splurge a little if you can and get a nice one. It's a big day. And you'll definitely want to take the day off work. It's a very intense, very spiritual experience. You won't be able to just go back to work afterward. You'll want to spend the day in quiet reflection."

By that point in our Jewish education, we knew to take everything she told us with a big box of kosher salt. Still, when Ruth asked if anyone had any questions, any questions at all, about the elaborate and detailed process, I wanted to speak up. I couldn't, though, as I realized I had forfeited my right to do so when we missed the class field trip to the ceremonial baths. A query would have been met with a disapproving look and perhaps a cluck from our judgmental teacher.

Later, we asked our classmate Susan to fill us in on the big trip.

"It was nothing special, really," she said. "I expected a beautiful religious shrine, but it was like a whirlpool at a hotel, except with no jets."

Thankfully, we were given a handout on mikveh procedure. I found the answers to some of my questions contained within. The first proviso suggested that some people tried to get away with a simple toe-dip: "The <u>entire body</u> should be immersed at one time and <u>every part of the body</u> should be <u>in direct contact</u> with the mikveh <u>water</u>."

The underlining seemed gratuitous, but perhaps some smart aleck had tried to argue that immersion in drained mikveh still qualified under a previous set of less-exacting rules.

"Any separation between the skin and water renders the immersion invalid. Consequently, all dirt, cosmetics, nail polish, threads, hair pins, jewellery, dentures, contact lenses, Band-Aids, adhesions such as adhesive plaster, water repellent substances such as ointments, <u>MUST BE REMOVED!</u>"

The last time I had faced such a rule, I had secretly defied it. That was in the lab unit of my university organic chemistry class, where contact lenses were forbidden. The instructor wore the sort of giant spectacles that went out of style in the early 1990s, and it clearly wasn't a fashion choice. If you were to knock off your goggles and spray an organic solvent in your eye, we were warned, it could dissolve the plastic lens, glue it to your eyeball, blind you for life and leave you in a state of permanent crippling pain. On the other hand, it was a real hassle to have to remove my contacts in the middle of the day. I'm pretty sure that was my reasoning for disobeying the rules: convenience with maybe a smidgen of vanity. Thankfully, the sulphuric acid stayed in the beaker and I made it out with my eyesight intact.

This time around, faced with a similar no-contact edict, I decided to follow it. And that, ladies and gentlemen, is concrete proof that the third word in the title of this book is accurate. Nine years later, even without the threat of blindness, I'm able to follow simple instructions. Back then, I feared the lab instructor might come over and look me straight in the eye to check for the telltale ring around the pupil. This time, the overseer was God Almighty: He didn't have to do spot checks. Furthermore, my fears of being an imposter would actually be warranted if I wore my contacts. Without full immersion, I would never be Jewish.

The next set of rules concerned preparation, and they made working in a lab seem pretty tame. To be spiritually cleansed, you must first be physically scrubbed, according to the following method:

225

✡ Bathe entire body with hot water and soap—pay special attention to hairy regions of the body.

✡ Trim finger and toe nails to remove all dirt, torn cuticles and dried/loose skin.

✡ Clean nose and ears.

✡ There must be no food particles in teeth—either brush, use toothpick or dental floss and rinse mouth with water.

✡ Remove any dried blood from skin wounds by soaking in warm, soapy water.

✡ Shower with warm water followed by careful combing and brushing of hair. (We'd already bathed, but I assumed the extra shower was to drive the point home.)

✡ Make final inspection by tactile self-examination—pay special attention to removal of loose hair that may have fallen during the combing process.

Once your nose is thoroughly scrubbed of loose hairs, you make the big entrance. That part seemed pretty straightforward, but the instructions were nonetheless quite specific:

✡ Body should be relaxed, limbs slightly separated, eyes and lips gently closed.

✡ Avoid unnatural contortions.

✡ Immerse in a semi-squatting position—arms held away from the body.

✡ Immerse once, stand erect, eyes upward, arms folded beneath heart, and recite the Blessing.

✡ Immerse again.

Committing the prayer to memory was recommended but not required. That, I could do. We chose the day of the mikveh a month in advance, and when it arrived it was a clear but cold day in January. Sarah's sister Becky had left her car in our garage for the month, so we were able to drive up to the one bath that apparently served the whole city's Jewish community. Reform Jews, we had been told, didn't use it that often, while Orthodox Jews would use it any time they needed to purify themselves. The scheduling was tight, so we needed to be there at 11 on the dot.

Our rabbi was without wheels, so we arranged to pick him up in front of the synagogue. I double-parked while Sarah ran in, and I sat there, car running, just a guy listening to classic rock and reviewing his prayers before he got naked in front of community elders. It felt a little weird, but only a little.

"All ready for the mikveh?" the rabbi asked as he got in the car.

"I think so! I have my robe, as Ruth advised."

"Okay," he said in a tentative way he'd likely developed after counselling hundreds of awkward teens on their way to bar and bat mitzvahs.

"Uh, she said it's important to bring a robe."

"Well, it can't hoyt," he said in his mock New Yorkese. I remembered the phrase from our first meeting and smiled.

We headed north on Bathurst Street, Toronto's boulevard of Jewish history. It begins downtown, where our shul is one of the few left, and progresses up a hill and over a ravine to the large, affluent temple that is the city's biggest. In a strip mall just north of there, we picked up our witness.

"Can I get a witness!?" the faux James Brown song in my head cried—a faux Marvin Gaye, technically—but I did my best to block it out. The man in question, chosen by our rabbi, was a longtime member of the shul, though I'd never seen him before. I wondered if he'd been in the gym on Yom Kippur, or whether he was observant enough to attend the main event. There was also the possibility that I didn't recognize him because we had been so lax in our synagogue attendance, a thought that gave me a tinge of guilt. Ultimately, though, I was glad to have a witness I didn't recognize.

We said hello, and he and the rabbi took the back seat while my fiancée and I switched seats. With Sarah driving and me riding shotgun, it was like we were taking the kids to soccer practice, only the kids were our spiritual elders. They talked about temple business in the back, and I kept my eyes on the road and monitored Sarah's driving.

"Now there's still the business of the $100 mikveh fee," the rabbi leaned forward to say. "I mention it because we're going to be passing the rabbinate offices where we can stop and pay."

"I'm sorry, I think I forgot to bring the cheque," I said, mildly annoyed with myself. "I brought my comfortable robe as per Ruth's recommendation but forgot about the whole price of admission part."

"I might have it in cash," Sarah said. "Check in my purse."

I pulled out her bacon wallet, a gag gift from a friend that looks remarkably like a billfold of raw pork slices. I realized what I was holding and suddenly became quite concerned that the rabbi had seen it as well. It was one thing not to keep kosher, but to wave around a *traif* wallet in front of your religious leader seemed too brazen, especially in these last hours of my gentile life. I shoved the wallet back in Sarah's purse.

"You know what, why don't we stop at this ATM?" I said. "I need to get money anyway."

A block north was the headquarters of the Canadian Council for Reform Judaism, the same squat office building in which I had faced down the *beit din* a few weeks before. While the rabbi ran in to make the deposit, I tried to make small talk with my fellow congregant.

"So, have you been a member of the synagogue long?"

"Yes, about twenty years."

"And do you come to a lot of these, uh, mikveh visits?"

"When I'm asked."

It was about as awkward as our conversations with our suspected Mossad agent driver. The rabbi returned and we continued northward, eventually arriving at a suburban Jewish elementary school. It didn't seem like the right place, but the rabbi headed in purposefully. With robe, slippers and towel in hand, I followed.

There we met Bruce, a temple elder I recognized. He was the good-natured president of the shul and he half-heartedly grumbled about the security sign-in we had to pass through.

"The day we have to sign in at our temple . . ." he said to the rabbi.

"Well, you know how they are with security," the rabbi replied, again in that way that implied he didn't agree but wouldn't actually come out and say it. I realized it was this ability to say things without saying them—those who understand, understand—that made him so good at his job.

We proceeded through the locker-lined halls and down the stairs, and I felt briefly like I was regressing. The mikveh was in the basement, at the end of a hall of classrooms, which seemed like an odd location until I realized there were strict rules about how the water could arrive in the small pool. It had to be stationary, natural water, meaning from a spring or the rain, and it couldn't come through a tap. It could travel through a pipe as long as the pipe was open on both ends, and only gravity could propel it. I wasn't sure how they would clean the pool, but it was clear the kids weren't allowed in during gym class.

Behind the first door was a waiting room of the sort you'd find in a doctor's office. Thankfully, it was empty. I removed my shoes and socks while the rabbi and witnesses prepared the necessary forms.

"Now, Sarah," the rabbi said, "only men are allowed in the mikveh room when a man is being immersed, but there's a vent in the wall in the office next door. You can sit there and listen to the whole thing."

"All right, Ben, we're ready when you are," the rabbi said. I walked through the next door to a small, tiled room with a small, step-in pool on one side. It looked most immediately like a hospital facility, the sort of place where they would help injured football players learn to walk again. I was motioned toward the next door, which led to a change room and shower. I disrobed, took out my lenses, showered, shampooed and checked my teeth in the mirror for any conversion-voiding flecks of food. There were none.

Spurning my robe, I wrapped my towel around my waist, took a deep breath, exited the antechamber and padded over to the pool. The three wise men—not the right reference, I know, but that's what they were—had assembled.

"Sarah, can you hear us?" the rabbi asked.

"Yes," her muffled voice responded.

"Okay, let's begin," he said.

I hung the towel on the hook and stepped into the water. It was comfortably warm and I walked the rest of the way in. I then began the three immersions, clutching knees to chest as if doing a cannonball. I plunged down as far as I could, worried that my back might have stayed above water. None of the blurry figures I could make out said anything upon my resurfacing, so down I went, again and again.

Then came the prayer, which had been freshly rinsed out of my mind. The rabbi, ready for this, held up a laminated prayer card the size of a placemat. I could make out the Hebrew, just barely, but wasn't in a state to read it. My squinting made this clear and I repeated the prayer after the rabbi.

Then came the Statement of Gerut, or conversion. It makes sense, I thought at the time, to have people make solemn oaths while standing naked in a pool of water. You can't feel much more vulnerable. I repeated after the rabbi, in English this time.

Of my own free will I choose to become a Jew.

I hereby affirm my faith in Judaism alone and dedicate myself to joining with the Jewish people in their struggle for freedom and justice for themselves and all others.

*I commit myself to the ongoing pursuit of Jewish know-
ledge. My home will be one where Jewish tradition and
learning are honoured and sustained. If I am blessed with
children, they will have the benefit of a Jewish upbringing.
I will participate in the life of the synagogue and of the
Jewish community.*

This was as solemn a vow as I had ever made. Not going to
shul, becoming a High Holidays–only Jew, would be breaking
it. I took a deep breath and continued.

*I pledge to dignify my life by incorporating into it those
life cycle events which bind me to God and Klal Israel.*

At that point, I was to sing the Shema, the holiest prayer
in Judaism and the one that, when I heard it in temple, still
gave me a slight shiver, the closest thing I felt to an inexplicable
spiritual feeling. I still had water in my ears, I told Sarah later,
when she asked why I sang it so loudly. Though that was true,
I was also eager to prove my mastery of a prayer that was as
important as it was simple.

Shema Israel! Adonai Elohenu! Adonai Ehad!

A few more lines of prayer were read, and I had that familiar flicker for what would be the last time. Isn't this weird?
it asked. You're standing naked in front of three men, two of
whom you barely—and I know my subconscious intended
the bad pun—know, in the basement of a school, chanting an

ancient language. To an uninitiated observer, it was weirder than Yom Kippur but not quite as weird as the mohel, but I was no longer that observer.

I stepped out, put my towel on and exchanged *mazel tovs* with my rabbi and the witnesses and Sarah's muffled voice through the wall. I showered, briefly panicking when I turned the water on—was it a sign of disrespect to take a profane shower after a sacred dip? They never mentioned it, so I figured it was safe to assume that it wasn't. Then I dressed and exited to the office, where Sarah kissed me as a Jew for the first time and I signed the official log. I'd never worn the robe. Silly Ruth.

"You know, when I converted, I had a real hard time with the immersions," the temple president said. "I think I'm naturally too buoyant. I just couldn't get myself completely under." I was thankful both for my lack of buoyancy and the fact that I hadn't heard that story before I took the plunge.

Our rabbi hitched a ride back to the city with the temple president, and we took the taciturn witness home. He revealed that he was a poet, and somehow this was reassuring. Once we dropped him off in Forest Hill, we were ready for my first official meal as a Jew. Yitz's Delicatessen, a landmark restaurant famous for its door handles that look like giant sausages, was our choice, and it did not disappoint. I had a smoked meat sandwich with fries, coleslaw, a kosher dill and a glass of Vernor's ginger ale, while Sarah opted for a scoop of egg salad on a bagel, augmented with bites of my sandwich.

"So, how do you feel?" Sarah asked.

"Well, squeaky clean," I replied, "but also relieved. It's all done now. I made it."

"All done except for the wedding."

"Oh right, that little event. Honestly, though, that's the party. We've done the hard part."

"I like that. If it's just a big party, we can now officially relax."

As we reclined in our seats, Sarah spotted a respected septuagenarian author enjoying lunch over his newspaper, and took that as a sign that we were in the right place.

Unlike Moe Pancer's, this restaurant was bustling, relatively centrally located and, if not hip, then at least not past its prime.

She took out her camera to capture the moment. She started to laugh, but caught herself before it was audible.

"What?"

"You know the famous author sitting behind you?"

"Yes."

"Well, he just left to go to the bathroom—and he's taking his pickle with him!"

I swivelled to look, and sure enough I saw him shuffling to the back of the restaurant, arms behind his back and kosher dill in hand. Such are the sights these Jewish eyes have seen.

Jew, Me?

Was my goal all along to become a Jew or to become a Lazarovic? This question came up in a conversation with Ryan, and while I thought the answer was clear, he assured me it was not.

Why did I do this? Was it that I loved their Florida family jam sessions so much that I wanted in? Not really, though I enjoyed trying to keep a beat on the tambourine. Was it that I was eager to have Jake and Debbie to call upon for advice when I needed it? No, I could do that without changing religions. Rather, Ryan's point was that, in a sense, marriage is a conversion.

"When I married Marie, I converted to being French," he explained quite matter-of-factly. "It wasn't a course or any sort of program, obviously, but the effect was the same. I learned how to drive like a Frenchman—well, I'm probably the soberest man behind the wheel in Corsica, but you know what I mean.

I use the French technique of cutting to the front of the line when I can. And I certainly appreciate the French attitude toward wine."

The Ryan I went to university with would frequently preface his observations with the phrase, "Now, I'm just a boy from Saskatchewan . . . ," a sort of homage to Diane Keaton's character in *Manhattan* who, by way of explaining how shocked she was by modern mores, would say, "I mean, really, I'm just from Philadelphia." (Having been to Ryan's hometown of Prince Albert, I can assure the people of Philadelphia they have nothing to worry about.) He used to drive the speed limit, and on one occasion pulled over on the side of the 401 to adjust his seat belt, something that just isn't done on one of the busiest highways in North America.

But that had changed. Now he wore fancier ties and more stylish glasses. He also spoke fluent French. Admittedly, he still enjoyed things like the store-bought mayonnaise Marie wouldn't allow in the house, but that was the beauty of marriage, he explained.

"I'm still a Saskatchewan boy at heart, you see, but now I'm perfectly comfortable in Paris or Corsica or Normandy," he said at the culmination of one of his Carlo Rossi–fuelled philosophical dialogues. "And Marie has some idea of what life is like in Prince Albert, where my grandfather refers to his collection of *National Geographic*s as 'booooks' and orders a coffee with his Whopper. We both have some understanding of another way of life, and perhaps feel somewhat more at home in another place. And that, dear Ben, is why you should get married. Now, how about another round of that fine Mr. Rossi?"

All of his points were excellent ones, and not just because they were explained over a jug of cheap red wine. Still, I was now something more than a future husband. I was a Jew. What did this mean? Despite the claims of the anti-Semites, it sadly did not give me the power to control world events. That said, membership does have its privileges.

One is joining a select club that has its own holidays and language. Like the Masons, it gives you reason to be proud of all the accomplished people who have come before you. To wit, there's the near-cliché "Did you know he's one of us?"—something that was already familiar to me as a Canadian. (As in, did you know the inventor of basketball was Canadian? Well, he came up with the game in Massachusetts, but sure.)

"Paul Newman was Jewish, you know," Sarah's uncle Michael told me after the actor died.

"Wasn't he half?" I said, summoning the lyrics of Adam Sandler's Hanukkah song from the recesses of memory.

"Maybe, but he starred in *Exodus,* so that's 50 percent plus one right there."

Such were tribal loyalties.

Of course, the much more important benefits are the simple, subtle comforts of religion. I now had a set of rules by which to live my life. Even if I didn't follow them, they were there.

This satisfaction offered by religion isn't well advertised— why sell something as dull as peace of mind when you can promise eternal salvation?—but it exists. I'm under no illusion that Judaism has a monopoly on these comforts, and it certainly takes nothing away from my affiliation to say that.

I realized as much in conversation with Tristan, my soon-to-be-married friend and squash partner. He was as lax a Lutheran as I was a Catholic, but to be married in the church, he and his fiancée had to attend an education seminar. He dreaded it beforehand, suspecting it would be filled with young meatheads pushed into something they didn't understand. That was partly the case, but the priest in charge was much wiser than he had expected.

Tristan summed up his lesson for me: "You know, even if you don't believe in God, even if you just think Jesus was a historical figure who had visions, you have to admit he did good," he said between puffs of a post-squash cigarette. "To spread a pretty uniformly positive message that lasted thousands of years—even if it was often corrupted—is amazing in its own right."

That's when I realized how petty some of my disagreements with Catholicism were, and how many of the conclusions I've drawn from Judaism might just as easily been drawn by another person from another religion. It was a natural part of the conversion process to convince myself that this new religion was vastly superior to what I knew before—and in some ways I remain convinced that it is. But now I can see that the framework I found was much bigger than any one faith.

The more I thought about it, the more I decided that religion is too comforting, useful and life-affirming to be left to the wingnuts. It's like the wedge issues in modern elections: there's a broad consensus on so many things, but the greasy opportunists pick divisive issues to manufacture victories by chipping away at what we agree on rather than building on it. Atheism, at least the sort espoused as a none-of-the-above default by people like me, is an obvious but unfortunate solution. Though it doesn't fit my case, you could say it's throwing baby Jesus out with the bathwater.

After ignoring the loudmouths, the previously put off should remember that no one can stop them from practising religion the way they want. Nothing turns a free-thinking, intelligent person off like unsupported instructions on how to behave. The mandate not to cherry-pick—one that all religions, to a degree, have to enforce in order to keep things together— is intrinsically flawed. Every faith has cast aside inconvenient tenets at some point, and there's no justification for not extending this freedom to all. Some may insist on a Christmas tree at Hanukkah, and while that's fine with me, both religions are justified in strictly forbidding it. If that confused worshipper finds some solace in lighting candles and vacuuming up pine needles, so be it. Obviously, there are limits on this ad-libbing, and religious institutions should trust intelligent, honest worshippers to respect them. Between the many different shuls of Jewish thought, the many looser sects of Christianity and every other variant of faith that exists, there's plenty of room for personal interpretation of religion. There's also no reason to forgo the very basic human desire to—if you want to, if you can, and only if you can—believe.

Stronger still, at least for me, was the desire to belong. I knew for certain that I did when I formed a *minyan* for the first time.

I was rushing from work to temple on the second Friday night of the month. Sarah was simultaneously headed to shul from her home office. During class, our attendance had been mandated. Now, I went both because I had made my vow in the mikveh and because, finally, it was beginning to feel like the right thing to do. As our rabbi had told us early on, the more you put in, the more you'll get out. That had initially seemed like circular logic—any complex activity you dedicate yourself to will eventually make more sense. But as a way to wind down the work week, a religious service made sense. I knew the songs, could read some of the prayers, recognized faces and, most important, was engaged by the rabbi's sermons.

On this particular Friday, I was fifteen minutes late. When I entered the synagogue, the rabbi came up to me, smiled, shook my hand, wished me good shabbas and thanked me for forming the *minyan*. I was the tenth Jew, thus the one who rounded out the quorum necessary to have God dwell among the congregants, allowing the service to begin. It felt good.

Though my comfort with Judaism was important, our looming wedding quickly became the priority. Debbie had found us a Montreal rabbi to do the deed, one who had the distinction of having married our Toronto rabbi. We visited Montreal to meet him, and on that occasion he interviewed us both and asked what we saw in one another. It seemed silly at first, as bold questions often do, but it was as revealing as it was simple.

I began: "In Sarah, the first thing I saw was a creative mind, someone who comes up with brilliant and sometimes loopy ideas that I often wish I'd had. Obviously, I also saw the body that mind inhabited, and that just sealed the deal. She's a kind, caring, funny and extremely intelligent woman, and that's why I love her. That, and she has the good sense to love me."

Of course, following my lead was easier, but Sarah still managed a convincing answer: "In Ben, I also have someone very smart and creative, but more important than that, someone who cares a great deal for the people around him. He calls his grandmothers every Sunday, and takes good care of his mother and brother and sister. He's always thinking about making other people happy. He's the most thoughtful person I know."

Was that it, then? I wasn't sure whether an off-the-cuff answer was the truest one or merely the most immediately available. I was happy with Sarah's answer, and she with mine, but at the same time I was glad we didn't have to do this sort of thing very often. It also reminded me that I had a reputation to live up to.

The rabbi then ran through a list of Jewish wedding traditions, asking us which we would like to observe. We wavered between trying to gauge his opinions about which were important and worrying about a ceremony that more than half the attendees likely wouldn't understand.

And then there was the issue of keeping it short and sweet. Most Jewish weddings happen on Sunday, as the Sabbath is off limits. As we were already asking nearly all our guests to travel a considerable distance, I didn't think we could make them skip a day of work as well. That meant waiting until nightfall on the Saturday, a proposition made trickier by the fact that we opted to wed on one of the longest days of the year. This meant the whole ceremony, dinner, speeches, dancing and party—the culmination of more than a year of planning—would be compacted into five short hours. We were ready.

Crunching the Light Bulb

I was prepared to take Sarah to be my lawful wedded wife, but that wasn't nearly enough. Our wedding, which we had idly imagined as a big party with family and friends, had begun to balloon into something beyond our control.

Which was fine, we thought, because from the beginning Debbie had volunteered to steer the beast. She arranged everything and spent the final month finessing every detail. In the twenty months of our engagement, she had treated every wedding she attended as an opportunity for reconnaissance: What did they do right? What did they do wrong? What ideas should be borrowed, adapted or quashed before they arose?

She would run her findings by Jake and us—Team Wedding—apologizing in advance for her attention to detail.

Sarah, I know you probably think this over the top, but I'd really like to make loot bags for the hotel rooms of the out-of-town guests with things like maps and bottles of water so they don't have to use the minibars. I went to one wedding where the bride and groom's pictures were put on special chocolate bars, and I'd like to do that, too. Can you send me a picture of you and Ben? And what do you think about designing the bags? xoxoxoxoxo Mom.

We would ever-so-gently tweak these requests to better reflect our sensibilities. We drew the line at bag design, only because we couldn't think of a design that both my grandmothers and our friends would use. We did offer a compromise on the chocolate bars: Sarah offered to illustrate a handwritten wrapper for them. It read

Thank you: For helping me build a trellis; for taking care of that dumb cat; for introducing me to The Big Lebowski; *for commenting on my blog; for being a terrific colleague; for bringing over the bubbly; for the challah board; for bringing us to a meat draw; for being a great cook; for being a prune; for laughing at me laughing at my own jokes; for putting us up in London; for the burbchomps; for the curling win; for the tiara; for the dance moves; for the Flaming Laszlos; for being you; for the flu shot; for nursing me to health when I got food poisoning in Egypt; for helping me know my bubby better; for being my grandmother; for blowing up the balloons; for coming all the way from Florida;*

for helping me get through high school; for gracing our basement with your stuff; for manning the BBQ; for the legal advice; for the Hanukkah party jams; for being a cousin buddy; for the literary conversations; for the bon mots; for the late-night chats; for teaching me right from less-right; for the production nights; for kayak expeditions; for Balkan camp; for loving animals so I don't have to; for coming to our wedding and dancing all night!

Sarah and I had cross-checked the guest list several times to come up with just the right mix of inside jokes and generalities that would make everyone feel special but not too special. In doing so, we realized just how massive the guest list had become: the room's capacity was 150 and we were nudging the limit.

As per Laurette's demand, The Professor was hosting a garden party the night before the wedding. This occasioned a complete landscaping of the backyard of his large Westmount semi, a project my mother insisted was past due. She also insisted upon having a mariachi band, a surreal touch that I assumed to be a joke until I realized she was dead serious.

Jake was understandably surprised by this development.

"Is there a Mexican theme I don't know about?" he asked Team Wedding on a conference call. "Will there be Tex-Mex food? It can be quite messy, you know."

"I actually have my heart set on a giant bean trough," I deadpanned. "I think my family would really appreciate that. Though we will need bibs."

Our family had no special connection to the traditional music of the Mexican street performers and, as far as I knew, this was an idea my mother had had, and that was that. That determination made me proud to be her son.

A month before the big day, the pressure started to mount.

My brother—who was my best man—started having nightmares related to my wedding, which he shared with my mother and me over email.

"I had a bad dream last night that I showed up at Ben's wedding in a tee-shirt and jeans, and was supposed to bring the wedding ring but forgot it on the train. I felt so stressed when I woke up," he wrote. A week later, another missive: "I had a dream last night that Ben bought Mum a trip to Las Vegas for Mother's Day, but he booked the trip for the same day as his wedding. It was tense."

I laughed it off then, but I soon realized he wasn't alone.

"Ben, do you think I'll need a hat for the wedding?" my mother phoned me at work to ask.

"Uh, I don't think so. It's not the Royal Ascot. It's low-key, remember. Low-key."

"I just don't want to get there and see all the other women with hats and I don't have one."

"Okay, I'll make sure none of the women wear hats. It'll be fine."

"What if Josh forgets his shoes?"

"What?"

"Remember at Carolyn's wedding? We were driving down to Smolkin's an hour before the ceremony because he only had sneakers. He needs to bring his dress shoes. Does he even have dress shoes?"

"Mom, that was ten years ago. He has dress shoes. It'll be fine."

"What time is the Saturday service? I don't think anyone knows when it is."

"It's at 11, I think, but I'll tell everyone. It's just a blessing, though. No one has to come. Completely optional. Low-key."

"What about food? Do we still not know how many people are coming? I need to give the caterers numbers."

"You'll know as soon as we do. Don't worry, it'll be fine."

When I finally got off the phone, I realized my heart was racing.

I emailed Sarah a partial transcript of our conversation.

"Saturday service is 10:30, all info on website," she wrote back. "No hat. Who cares if Josh forgets his shoes? Food: Should we assume those who haven't replied aren't coming? NO STRESS! Just tell your mom to keep calm and do yoga. Just talked to Debbie, who is surprisingly chill. Also, Lou the florist just called, he's great. Everything is going to be fine. Actually, great."

I took a deep breath. I knew my mother had the night before under control and Debbie had the night of, but I didn't realize that my mother considered me the go-between. Sarah had been charged with harassing those who didn't RSVP—we had foolishly forgotten to put a reply-by date on the invitations—and a final tally of guests was drawn up. I emailed the spreadsheet to my mother, unaware that while the bill for catering and live music was adding up, the landscaping of the yard had yet to come together. From Vermont, my mother tried to move this along on weekends, but being out of the country didn't help. We had originally guessed that half the guests would make the Friday night dinner. Now, it was looking more like two-thirds, which meant a hundred people—a few of whom were related to my mother, a scattering of young people she didn't know, a bunch of relatives of my father she hadn't seen since the divorce and a huge congregation of Lazarovic friends, family and acquaintances.

My mother likes to entertain small groups and does her best to avoid crowds. These underlying traits, combined with a mud pit in the yard, a remarkably expensive group of Hispanic troubadours and a long list of names she either didn't know or had blocked from her memory, triggered what she would refer to as a hairy canary.

I could sense the hyperventilation in the email: "I am feeling a little out of the loop. I am providing food and drinks to people I don't have a clue about. Who are these people I am spending so much on? Could you give us a clue?"

I called her immediately, but not before she called Debbie, a conversation that didn't go well. The details were sketchy (and for my mental health, I preferred to keep them that way), but my mother had said some unpleasant things. As I became more and more agitated, my low-key mantra fell by the wayside. There was a time to reiterate that you didn't care about the details as long as the important people were there, but three weeks from the wedding day wasn't it.

The conversation, which took place on the outside steps of my office, was no one's finest moment, though in retrospect it was a good opportunity to burn off all the accumulated tension.

"Son," my mother said, her voice wavering, "I think you've been really quite rude to me throughout this whole planning. Everyone has taken me for granted."

"I was rude to you? I was rude to *you?* You just called Debbie and set a new standard for rudeness! Oh, and excuse me for being otherwise occupied planning *my wedding!*"

"Of course, it's *your* wedding. It's all about you. Don't worry about anyone else!"

I started sputtering, a sound I had never made before and hope never to make again. "For Christ's sake"—not using his name in vain anymore—"this is one day when it *is* all about me!"

This discussion continued over the course of four phone calls, each of which ended with her hanging up and me angrily calling her again. The end result was my acceptance of her escalating threats to cancel the garden party, boycott the wedding and ensure that her whole side of the family stayed home.

"Well, the good news is, there will be plenty of extra chocolate bars," I told Sarah before laying out the precipitous turn of events.

That evening, my sister happened to call my mother to ask about makeup plans for the wedding and was surprised to hear that the mother of the groom was no longer planning to attend. In yet another violation of the divorced children's pact to limit each parent's knowledge of the other parent's activities—though, given the circumstances, this one was understandable—Jasmine told my father what had happened. He had been receiving periodic planning calls from Jake until this time and was helping to keep things running smoothly. He called as soon as he heard.

"I'm sorry about what happened with your mother," my father said over the phone. "If there's anything I can do to help, just let me know."

Though I appreciated the offer, I knew that if my mother saw my father doing anything to fill the void, it would just look like the sabre-rattling before the nuclear war began.

"Thank you for that," I said, suddenly wishing I could take back my groomzilla rant. "And thanks for all your help with the wedding. I'm sure everything will work out fine."

I wasn't really sure, of course, as it seemed pretty intractable. My brother tried to mediate, but he was too close and too tense to have much success. And that's when Ryan came through for us.

Back in university, whenever my mother would call, I would invariably be working at the student paper. She would end up getting Ryan on the horn, and in his advanced state of procrastination he would chat with her for hours. I wasn't thinking of that tendency under these circumstances, of course; I only thought that, since he was acting as my MC, I could, as a last resort, redirect the mariachi band and caterers to his backyard.

A day after I made that request, my mother called. The purpose of the call was neither an apology nor an explanation, but rather a comparison that put everything in perspective. Ryan had called her and, in a weird way, set things right.

"Ryan told me about his wedding," she said. "I had no idea his mother locked up the house and checked into a hotel under an assumed name in a different city three days before the ceremony."

"Yeah, it was something," I responded cautiously.

"I guess it makes this look pretty silly, huh?"

"A bit. I'm sorry, Mom. I know I'm putting you under a lot of pressure and I want you to know I appreciate it."

She accepted the apology, but really just wanted to recount the many gory details of Ryan and Marie's wedding. As talk therapy, it worked wonderfully. I realized that, as a guest at his wedding, I had little inkling that anything was wrong. This, in turn, calmed me down.

A week later, things were back on track. And then Baby Sofia was born.

She was underweight, red as a beet and would be staying in the neonatal unit for the foreseeable future. She was also healthy and had been delivered without complication. Mitze was thrilled, my father was relieved and Debbie quickly sent several CDs of children's music from around the globe. As we visited Baby Sofia—"Why do we say 'Baby' Sofia?" I asked Josh. "It's not like we know other Sofias. It makes her sound like she was rescued from a well on CNN"—I pulled my middle two siblings aside and pleaded for message control on this one.

"The baby's here, she's healthy and all is good, but there's no need to tell Mom unless she asks, okay? There's a lot to pull together in the next few days and we need to stay focused." They agreed.

Indeed, my mother did display a laser-like focus. Two weeks before the wedding weekend, the landscapers were nowhere to be seen. Acting quickly, The Professor brought in a new team he rustled up from parts unknown and instilled the fear of God in them. Based on the speed at which topsoil and patio brick was laid, they did indeed believe in the higher power The Professor cited. With every square foot of yard reclaimed from the mud pit, I could hear the strain lessen in my mother's voice.

With that under control, I turned my attention to the only task for which I was wholly responsible: the cake. To maintain my stress-reduction initiative, I quickly outsourced this job to Marie. She was a francophone on the ground in Montreal, so it seemed logical. What made the task considerably more complex was my insistence on a cake made of concentric wheels of fine cheeses.

I had read that a local chef had made such a thing at his wedding and I immediately saw three huge advantages. First, we would have the rare opportunity to be high rollers at one of the city's best cheese shops. Second, it was guaranteed to be a better dessert than a regular wedding cake. In the annals of sweets, few pastries match the traditional tiered white cake for both effort expended and taste buds disappointed. The tradition of giving keepsake pieces to guests—anything to get rid of it—confirms this. Third, it was a guaranteed conversation starter, and a cross-cultural one at that. With my western Canadian relatives mixing with Sarah's Israeli cousins and a sizable contingent of Boca Ratonians—not to mention my parents' respective and possibly less-than-respectful families—having a conversation piece at the centre of the table would be a mitzvah. On our special day, we decided we would happily choose cut-the-cheese jokes over awkward conversation.

Marie successfully explained all this to the head of the cheese department at La Vieille Europe. With some assurance from me that the order was for real, we arranged to see the cheese two days before the wedding. Into the catacombs of the store we went, passing secret delicacies as we descended to the temple of cheese. Gleefully, he pulled out wheel after wheel of fragrant excess, offering a tame, mild choice and a more pungent one, then offering his respectful praise when we opted for the latter. A thousand dollars later, we had an impressive stack of the wine of foods, starting with a giant Pecorino, then a Jarlsberg for the Manitoba relatives, then a big Stilton, and on up to the crowning Époisses. This, he said when it was all selected, is a real work of art. Indeed, it was the best possible display of the food that is milk's leap to immortality, something that would have made the responsible cows, sheep and goats beam with pride.

The day of the mariachi dinner was glorious. We had left the purchase of the rings until then and spent the morning trying to figure out where one bought such items at a minimal markup. Ryan and Marie had picked theirs up at Walmart, so I saw a perfect opportunity to visit Costco. Unfortunately, there were no gold bands to be had at my favourite big-box retailer. We found a jewellery store in the basement of a downtown mall and had the bands resized by mid-afternoon. Though we were slightly embarrassed at first at how little we paid, Sarah reminded me that we had Jewish custom on our side: the wedding band is supposed to cost the equivalent of a *prutah,* the smallest coin in ancient Israel and one that could get you a tenth of a loaf of bread. Our rings, while inexpensive, cost considerably more than that.

When I arrived at The Professor's, the patio was intact, the caterers were set up and the mariachi band had just arrived. As our host tamped down stray bits of sod, the five musicians strode to the centre of the yard, their silver charro outfits glimmering in the late-day sun. They began to play, not "La Cucaracha" as

I realized I had been expecting, but an even faster song. The Professor's sod stomping looked like the appropriate dance for the music, so I joined in. He was grinning beatifically.

"This must be a first for the neighbourhood," I shouted to him.

"Pardon?"

"I say, this must be a first for the neighbourhood."

"Oh no," he said. "We had a mariachi band here at the house for Al's sixteenth."

The fact that he'd done this before for his daughter's birthday only impressed me more; this wasn't a spur-of-the-moment thing my mother had dreamed up, but rather their over-the-top way of marking special occasions. I felt honoured to be a part of the tradition of sombreros.

My mother's early concerns about food were accurate: a huge number of guests came and cleaned out the caterers. It didn't matter, though. Everyone who ate was sated, and those who didn't could take it as a reminder to be on time the next night.

I knew the intermingling of Florida Jews, my two grandmothers and our friends would be an odd one, but I suppose my imagination hadn't played the appropriate Mexican soundtrack. My mother gritted her teeth and played superhostess, zeroing in on confused-looking Erretts who hadn't seen her in more than a decade and giving them the warmest welcome she could muster. When sundown arrived, Debbie gathered the Jews inside for a spirited lighting of the Shabbat candles. With all the Lazarovics together, it quickly turned into a rousing singalong to rival the one outside. Curious gentiles, The

Professor among them, wandered in and joined in the joyous singing of "Shabbat Shalom."

The next day began not with a bang but an *aufruf.* This was one of the traditions we opted to observe, and not only because it was fun to say. It consisted of being called up to the Torah during Shabbat services before the wedding, a nice way to see what our Montreal rabbi did when he wasn't presiding over weddings. It was also a good introduction to Judaism for my family, none of whom had set foot in a synagogue before.

That morning's services included the bat mitzvah of a young lady who, the rabbi gently told us in advance, would have had everything in pink if she could. The Torahs were not dyed for the occasion. The girl-turned-woman acquitted herself quite nicely, but her parents made long, inappropriate speeches that reached their pinnacle when her father explained how, though he loved his little princess, he'd really wanted a boy.

"When she was born," he told the assembled congregation, which included Sarah's family and my brother and mother, "I had to double-check the genitals to make absolutely sure it wasn't a boy."

I felt a rush of relief that we hadn't told more guests about this part of the weekend. I looked back to see my brother with his head in his hands and my mother trying not to laugh.

The young woman's parents stumbled over their Hebrew at the podium, which only served to make me look like a professional. Sarah and I stood before the congregation and read from the Torah in perfect harmony. Well, we repeated after the rabbi in perfect harmony, but the point is we didn't flub our lines.

Afterward, Sarah was rushed off to a ladies' hair-and-makeup session, leaving me to my own devices for the afternoon. Just about everyone I knew was in this city, but I was alone. I quickly tracked down a group of friends enjoying dim sum in Chinatown and joined them for some sacri-licious dumplings. As I was still in my synagogue suit, I felt a bit like a visiting dignitary, and it was suggested that we try to get a free wedding-day meal out of La Maison Kam Fung, or at least a complimentary mango pudding. Neither happened. Later, with still more time on my hands, I purchased a special pair of red wedding socks and went for a run on Mount Royal (in non-wedding socks). As I was leaving the hotel, Sarah's aunt Janet grabbed my arm and implored me to be careful out there. With the sudden unwelcome thought of having to limp down the aisle in crutches, I took things nice and slow.

Once I returned, showered and tuxed up, it was go-time. The faculty club was just up the street from the hotel. I walked up alone. We assembled for pictures in the grand, wood-panelled lobby, distributed corsages and welcomed guests while waiting for the sun to set.

We had considered not seeing each other on the day of the wedding, but decided that was silly. Sarah did, however, manage to keep her dress under wraps until that moment. It was a vintage gold ballgown with matching tiara, and she glittered as she walked down the wide staircase.

"You look shiny," I said, momentarily at a loss for words. "Shiny beautiful, I mean!"

"You like this dress?" she said, wide-eyed.

"I love the dress," I replied. "Not as much as I love you, though. That would be weird."

Canapés were served, as was tropical punch that had been mislabelled as "torpical punch," allowing me to defuse the tension in the room—of which I was the primary repository—with an extraordinarily weak joke about it actually being *topical* punch that reflected the day's headlines.

Soon, we were summoned upstairs to the antechamber. The rabbi looked out the window and decided that three stars would have been visible if it weren't so cloudy. He officiated over *havdalah*, the prayers that separate Shabbat from the rest of the week. The spice box came out and the special intertwined candle was lit. As The Professor anxiously watched the smoke detector, we marked the separation of sacred and profane with a huge flame.

The *ketubah*, or marriage contract, was signed and witnessed, as was the government form. So far, so good. Next came a rundown of what was about to occur, at which point our lack of preparation became quite apparent.

Would Sarah circle me seven times as we stood before the rabbi? This tradition supposedly comes from Jeremiah 31:22, which states that "a woman shall go around a man," but the modern, egalitarian version involved each of us doing three and a half circles around the other. I was going to point out that this wouldn't get us back to where we started, but kept my mouth shut to keep things moving. Yes, we would circle.

Would we break a glass? This tradition was even more nebulous; the best explanation we had heard was that the noise was meant to scare demons away. More tenuous was the reasoning that it commemorated the destruction of the temple (so I'm stomping on the temple?) or that it represented the bride's hymen (again with the inappropriate stomping). On the plus side, it would wake up sleeping relatives and add some action to the ceremony, so we acquiesced.

Ryan and Marie were the head *chuppah* holders. As Ryan and the rabbi fumbled with the telescoping aluminum poles required to hold the marriage canopy aloft, I had a vision of us all on a very awkward camping trip. Now the guests were waiting. Sandy may not have been the reason I converted, but she was incredibly helpful at a time when everyone was in a state of disarray. I realized my mother and father were both present, and the resulting tension seemed to slow all decision-making on everyone's part but Sandy's.

"All right, guys, it's time to go!" she barked, bringing the room to order. "Becky, Jane, down the aisle!"

Sarah's sisters went out the door and into the chapel, arm in arm. "Hi! Hi! Hello!" Jane said to the assembled guests as they turned to watch the procession.

My father, brother and sister went next, faces locked in nervous smiles. Then I walked my beaming mother down the aisle and turned to watch Debbie and Jake bringing Sarah to me.

Having heard Jane greet everyone was too much for Sarah. She began giggling uncontrollably. To sober her up, her father whispered to her, "Think of something serious! Think of Darfur!"

In addition to being highly inappropriate, this only made her laugh harder.

I spent most of the ceremony worried that my kippah was going to slide off, but when I wasn't worried about that, I took note of the rabbi's pitch-perfect, eloquent sermon. At one point, when he noted that, though we would only have our eyes on each other this day, we should and must look outward to the community as one, I made the two-finger I'm-watching-you gesture to Sarah, something she unfortunately missed because she was trying to figure out why one of our guests was climbing around a large potted plant. We later learned he was trying to get a perfect photo, though we have yet to see it.

The rings were exchanged, I kissed the bride and crushed the glass—a light bulb, I later learned, which makes for an odd heirloom—and it was official. We retreated to the antechamber and the guests were guided down to the ballroom. As we waited, I sprawled on the couch next to my wife.

"So now we're married."

"Yep."

"What a relief. Let's never do that again, okay?"

"Deal."

We kissed.

Our entrance to the ballroom inexplicably coincided with the playing of Sarah McLachlan's "Building a Mystery," a song I remembered as the very first entry on our do-not-play list. No one else in the room seemed to notice, so I said nothing. Dinner began immediately, as was necessary to pack a whole wedding into the time between sundown and our ejection from the venue at 1 a.m. Through sheer coincidence, the band redeemed itself by playing "All That Jazz" as light dinner music. This struck a musical-theatre chord with Sarah's aunts, who leaped out of their chairs to reveal an intimate knowledge of the choreography of *Chicago*. A small but enthusiastic portion of the Boca Raton delegation joined them. The room clapped along, our friends very much amused, my family somewhat confused and the waiters quite angry that all these jazz hands were preventing the mains from being served.

A married colleague had warned me that your wedding is a blur; having everyone you love in one room means you end up remembering nothing. Thankfully, knowing this seemed to prevent it from happening. I remember my speech and the groans I got for my admittedly bad joke about a Frenchman named Phillipe Phillope; I remember Jake explaining that, despite his early support of Hillary, he would be voting for Obama; I remember my father announcing that "Ben has a new baby sister, everyone"; I remember the club manager's shock at learning that a bottle of gin had disappeared shortly after a group of our under-refreshed friends were cut off by a surly bartender.

I remember our first dance, done to Harry Belafonte's "Jump in the Line," mainly for the element of surprise. I remember seeing Jake and Debbie hoisted up on chairs, looking a little wobbly but clearly used to the feeling. And I remember Sarah and me being lifted above the room on chairs and feeling much less secure than my new in-laws. From that perch, holding Sarah's hand, I could see Ryan and two of my three siblings among the team holding the chair from below, my mother and The Professor dancing the hora, my father and Mitze sitting with our cousins from Manitoba, my two grandmothers chatting amicably and Marie beginning the assembly of the cheese cake. The chair holders began to bob our chairs in time to the music, gently at first and then not so gently.

Sarah bounced along at roughly the same pace. She was laughing too hard to see me.

"Oy!" I yelled.

תודה רבה

Acknowledgements

I am indebted to my parents for making sure the right operation was performed at the right time and, more importantly, for their unwavering support. That goes double for their significant others, who weren't roped in by blood ties. Our good friends asked the many questions that made me think I should put it in writing. Jennifer Lambert and Sam Hiyate shaped some very raw copy. Dianna Symonds, Ken Whyte, Sarah Murdoch and Doug Kelly presented me with a series of wonderful career opportunities. Rohanna gave me the bacon wallet. Maryam and Jake read each draft. Rabbi Ed gave me his blessing. Tristan and Jeff took the heat when the cops showed up. And Sarah lived it.

The People of the Book have written some good ones on how to join their number, among them *Introduction to Judaism:*

A Sourcebook, compiled and edited by Stephen J. Einstein and Lydia Kukoff; *Living a Jewish Life* by Anita Diamant with Howard Cooper, as well as Diamant's *The New Jewish Wedding*. And every Jewish library ought to contain *Born to Kvetch* by Michael Wex, and *This Year in Jerusalem* by Mordecai Richler.

Names from the classroom and our trip to Israel were changed, though the characters were all too real.

Recipes

Sarah's mother, Debbie, and her aunt Sandy each have their preferred brisket recipe, but I've found it's better to take seconds than take sides. Writes Debbie, "The key to this recipe is cooking for two days, with lots of basting on the second day. Then let the brisket soak one more night and serve on the third day." Her recipe was passed down to her from Sonia Bank, the mother of her childhood friends Leslie and Andy Bank. Sandy's comes from the cookbook *Second Helpings* by Norene Gilletz (Canada's kosher queen!). "After trying so many recipes," Sandy writes, "this one has become the family favourite."

Debbie's Melt-in-Your-Mouth Brisket

4 TO 5 LBS BRISKET

2 ONIONS, SLICED

2 ENVELOPES OF LIPTON ONION SOUP MIX

GARLIC POWDER

HERBAL BOUQUET (FRESH BASIL, OREGANO AND ROSEMARY)

Day 1

1. Preheat oven to 350°F and Pam your pan.
2. Place brisket in pan, rub with garlic powder and add all other ingredients.
3. Fill pan with water until meat is half-covered.
4. Cover pan tightly with foil and cook for 4 hours.
5. Remove pan from oven and let cool to room temperature.
6. Wrap brisket in foil, pour gravy into jar and refrigerate.

Day 2

1. Preheat oven to 400°F.
2. Slice brisket on an angle as thinly as possible.
3. Cook slices in gravy for 4 hours, basting every 20 to 30 minutes. Skim off fat. Add a small amount of water if necessary to prevent meat from drying out or gravy from becoming too thick.

Day 3

1. Preheat oven to 350°F.
2. Heat brisket to desired temperature and serve.

Aunt Sandy's Best Brisket Ever

6 TO 8 LBS BRISKET

4 ONIONS

2 TSP SALT

FRESH PEPPER TO TASTE

1 TSP DRY MUSTARD

1 TBSP PAPRIKA

3 TBSP HONEY

1/2 CUP SOY SAUCE

4 OR MORE CLOVES OF GARLIC, CHOPPED

1. Chop onions coarsely and place in bottom of a foil pan.
2. In a bowl, mix salt, pepper, dry mustard and paprika.
3. Rub brisket thoroughly on both sides with the dry ingredients and place in pan.
4. In another bowl, mix honey, soy sauce and garlic.
5. Pour mixture over both sides of brisket.
6. Cover pan very tightly with tinfoil and marinate for at least 8 hours.
7. Bake at 325°F for 45 minutes per pound.

OUR ISRAEL ITINERARY